1/28/17

To Audrey,

From Carlsbad to

Petco Park!!...
Enjoy your Journey!

Your Fans,
The HoferKops

www.mascotbooks.com

Let's Hit 'Em All: A Family's Legacy Created Through Major League Baseball

For more information, please contact:
Mascot Books
560 Herndon Parkway #120
Herndon, VA 20170
info@mascotbooks.com

Library of Congress Control Number: 2016907884

CPSIA Code: PBANG0616A
ISBN-13: 978-1-63177-667-0

Printed in the United States

Let's Hit 'Em All

A FAMILY'S LEGACY CREATED THROUGH MAJOR LEAGUE BASEBALL

DAYNA & STEVE HAFERKAMP

FOREWORD BY *BUD BLACK*

Shoutouts from the Dugout

"Baseball has been a major part of my life as a fan, a player, and now a coach. It has shaped much of my life and my family's. It is an amazing game that should be shared by families for the history, the adventure, and all the lessons it teaches. I hope this book inspires you to spend time together and share those experiences."

Chad Moeller,
Former MLB catcher, World Series Champion

"Not many fans can claim they've taken down a Dodger Dog, a Fenway Frank, and everything in between in the same summer—and I'm sure Steve, Dayna, Grant, and Jack will remember the details of what they saw and learned together for the rest of their lives. I've known a lot of people over the years who have intended to do exactly what the Haferkamps did, only to abandon the plan a few ballparks in. To package a family journey around a summer-long ballpark pilgrimage may be the best route to discovery and bonding a family could ever take."

Matt Vasgersian,
MLB Network host

"I have been fortunate to be involved in professional baseball for forty-six years, fifteen as a player and thirty-one as a broadcaster. I have been able to play in many of the stadiums, mostly in the American League, and broadcast in most of the current stadiums, both new and old. I can only imagine what it would be like to be a young man, like Grant and Jack, and travel with my parents to see ALL the stadiums throughout Major League Baseball. They were able to see the new and old stadiums, sample the food, weather, and everything that makes each city so unique and do what many will be inspired to do after reading this wonderful book. Baseball has, and always will be, the one sport that everyone wants to somehow be a part of during their lifetime. I am very fortunate to be one of those."

Ray Fosse,
Oakland A's broadcaster, former MLB catcher

"The love for the great game of baseball starts with family and continues to evolve with each day's challenges, whether you are an aspiring player, coach, fan, or encouraging parent! The life lessons, the ups and downs, and the gamut of emotions, baseball continues to flourish! I have been blessed beyond belief to have baseball teach me the ways of life, all the while sharing all of it with my mom and dad and the rest of my loving family! Baseball is life and a passion of mine to share with fans just like the Haferkamps! Thank you for sharing your experiences and making this game of baseball America's pastime."

Mark Sweeney,
San Diego Padres broadcaster, former MLB player

"Here at the Rays, it's our mission to energize the community through the magic of baseball. The Haferkamps certainly understand that 'magic' of baseball. As a mother of two young boys who love the game, someday I can't wait to follow in the Haferkamps' footsteps and experience our national pastime with my family all across the country."

Melanie Lenz,
Tampa Bay Rays Senior Vice President of Strategy and Development

"Had a blast with Steve and his boys playing wiffle ball that day. One thing I've always had, since I can remember, is a love for the game. Steve and his family definitely have that and it is great to see. Thanks for letting me play, guys. It was fun."

Jerry Hairston, Jr.,
World Series Champion

"The game of baseball has been a major part of my life for as long as I can remember. I have fond memories of having a catch in the front yard with my dad trying to imitate my favorite player, All-Star catcher Thurman Munson of the New York Yankees. Throughout my playing years, as well as during my coaching career, I have been extremely fortunate to have been impacted by so many people, both on and off the field. I am looking forward to teaching my children more about the game that has been so special to me. Passing down the traditions and lessons of the game that I have learned is something that I value very much."

Kevin O'Sullivan,
University of Florida head coach

"Take it from the Haferkamps; baseball is a family tradition, and it can be with your family as well. I encourage all families to take part in an effort to bond not only with each other, but bond with the greatest game ever! Baseball and family... the ultimate double play! And who doesn't like a double play?"

Mud Grant,
San Diego Padres commentator and former MLB pitcher

"I have had the pleasure of knowing the Haferkamp family for the last six years and coaching their oldest son in youth baseball. Steve and Dayna are fantastic parents and their family's love for baseball combines two of the greatest American traditions: our national pastime and family. This is the story of how that love has been cultivated."

Erik Greupner,
Baseball executive, family friend

"A tip of the cap to the Haferkamps for *Let's Hit 'Em All*. Baseball has always been a big part of my family too. When I was a kid growing up in Ohio, my dad and I went to many Cleveland Indians games, and we watched the local Tribe telecasts together on hot summer nights. While the Indians were bad, we saw a lot of other really good teams and players up close. And there's no mustard in baseball that tops Bertman's ballpark mustard in Cleveland. I remember the first time I tasted it on a Cleveland Stadium hot dog. It was a Sunday afternoon doubleheader against the Red Sox. Amazing! Once I became a dad, I started taking my kids to MLB games because of the many great memories I had with my father. My kids and I have created many memorable moments from our visits to ballparks across the country. The best of all was an Arizona Spring Training vacation when we saw ten teams in six days! With the bonds we've created through baseball, my kids and I never run out of things to talk about. Inevitably, our conversations always seem to find a way of turning to the game we love. Baseball is how I connected with my father, and it became a great way for me to connect with my kids too."

Rick Redman,
Hillerich & Bradsby Co. VP Corporate Communications,
Makers of the Louisville Slugger

"I love the Haferkamps' spirit and Dayna's determination to chronicle their journey in *Let's Hit 'Em All*. It embodies many of the life lessons the game of baseball teaches us each and every season: perseverance, teamwork, discipline, and the ability to overcome adversity. It's also been my pleasure to coach their son Grant and form another lifelong relationship through the great game of baseball."

Chris Possemato,
Torrey Pines varsity pitching coach

"I always find it inspiring when a family has so much passion for the game of baseball to fully experience the sport throughout the country in various stadiums. The Haferkamps are true ambassadors of the game and their book will provide valuable insight to baseball fans everywhere."

David Rinetti,
Oakland A's Vice President of Stadium Operations

"Having the Haferkamps and Rebel Little League boys with the 2016 San Francisco Giants during Spring Training reminded me how special and humbling the game of baseball truly is. Those same eager eyes you see in those boys still exist even in our Big League players. The hope, thrill, and promise are common threads of all ages, and we were honored to have such a special group with us."

Bret Alexander,
San Francisco Giants Senior Director of Team Travel,
Home Clubhouse Manager

"As a Division I college coach at the University of San Diego, I have been fortunate to coach a lot of special talents. I also have coached Grant Haferkamp with the North County Mavericks development program. Regardless of age or level played, the journey the Haferkamps took on brings out the purist in a baseball fan. Enjoying the game of baseball as a family is truly a way to not only make some special memories but also use America's favorite pastime to forge a family bond."

Bradley Marcelino,
University of San Diego assistant coach

"As a former MLB catcher and current pro scout, I have had the privilege to visit 28 of the 30 current Major League Parks. To have the opportunity as a family to embark on this journey is remarkable and something they will never forget. The different ballpark cultures, the different foods, and the entire experience are any true baseball fan's dream. I have been fortunate enough to be part of this great game of baseball which has been good to me and my family. I can't wait to read about the Haferkamps' journey."

Kyle Phillips,
Former Toronto Blue Jays and San Diego Padres catcher,
current Chicago Cubs pro scout

"Baseball is a game of mental and physical sacrifice coupled with tons of failure! Why do we love this game so much?"

Justin Machado,
La Costa Canyon varsity head coach (3 CIF titles, 400+ wins)

"I've had the pleasure of knowing the Haferkamp family for many years. It has been my pleasure to visit with them at PNC Park, home of the Pittsburgh Pirates, several times and watch the Haferkamp boys grow up as well. Congrats on this wonderful journey and looking forward to the publication."

Donna Mangold,
Host at PNC Park and Three Rivers Stadium
for thirty-three seasons

"It was indeed my lucky day—first day on my new Spring Training job, first phone call, and I was very fortunate to meet the Haferkamps. What a wonderful friendship has been the result of one phone call. I love the picture album and look forward to the written word with pictures, as it will be an inspiration to many families—both young and old(er)! And to think I am a part of the Haferkamp legacy. What an honor. Thank you."

Linda Wyman,
Oakland A's

"Baseball has brought family and friends together and built unbreakable bonds. Relationships have been built around baseball from when I was a child and they remain today. My parents are no longer physical spectators of the sport, as their time on this Earth has passed. But I do know for fact that if anyone were to ask them today what some of their fondest memories were, they would tell you, undoubtedly, they were memories built around the baseball diamond, with family coming together and encouraging a young boy to swing hard, run hard, play hard, work hard, and respect the game."

Marc Lavoie,
University of Arizona baseball, private hitting coach for Grant and Jack

"The smell of a leather glove, the sound of a well hit ball, the taste of a hot dog, the feeling of a walk-off victory, and the sight of a freshly mowed ball field—does it get any better than this? The Haferkamps capture the energy and magnetism of our national pastime."

Pete Leddy,
Ph. D, Former Creighton University player, coach, and author

"It's been great following the travels of the Haferkamp family over the years. Seeing the boys grow up and hearing about all their adventures at other ballparks and spring training has been very entertaining. A favorite part of my job is to hear about everyone's favorite baseball memories and to see the passion and love for the game of baseball develop and be passed from one generation to the next. I feel fortunate to know this great family and glad to have them on board as Padres fans!"

Steve Carter,
Padres Manager of Membership Services

"My parents always told me that as a baby, I would pick up round objects and attempt to throw them. I guess that started my love for baseball. I played organized baseball as a youth through my career in the Army and well into my fifties, but I found a new love—coaching. I coached with Bob Shaw for about twenty years. Some of my players were Dante Bichette, Kevin O'Sullivan, and Nelson Rood. My love for the game continues as I still go to Roger Dean Stadium and wait for the cry, 'Play Ball!'"

Gene Meyerowich,
Longtime Jupiter area coach

"I have been a baseball player and fan in my early life and continued to be a baseball fan. I have been working for the Cincinnati Reds since 2009 in security for Spring Training. So, my association with baseball continues and enables me to meet and make friends with wonderful people."

Don Wyman,
Longtime baseball fan

"Baseball reflects life, especially considering the annual rebirth every spring and eventual death of most teams in the fall."

Steve Hargrave,
Former head coach of Dave Roberts at Rancho Buena Vista High

"I never really realized I fell in love with baseball until I started working for the Oakland A's. The relationships you create with people along the way are what make this game so special. To see and be a part of the Haferkamps' journey through the baseball world has been a remarkable experience. Over the last couple years I've been fortunate enough to have them be a part of what I call my baseball family."

Austin Ginn,
Oakland A's employee

"When I was twelve years old, I watched and listened to every single inning of the 1975 Detroit Tigers' season. They lost 102 games that year. It didn't matter. They were my team, and I loved them unconditionally. For the past forty years, I have tried to pass on that love and enthusiasm for baseball to my family and the players I have coached. I love how the game can connect communities and families like the Haferkamps. Their journeys exemplify everything that is great about baseball."

Jay Sill,
Family friend, longtime San Diego area coach

"I have had a love for sports since I was a little girl. I played all sports available: baseball, softball, basketball, track, and volleyball. After I suffered a career ending knee injury, I started on my passionate journey of coaching. I love coaching—coaching life, coaching morals, coaching responsibility. It is a chance for children to learn what it is to be a teammate, to be important, and to be a part of something great. My goal every day is to make each of my players feel like they are amazing, can do anything they set their minds to, and there is no limit to what they can accomplish if they only believe in themselves. I don't coach players...I coach people."

Jennifer Hayes,
Hartsburg Edmen state championship volleyball head coach

Don't get behind in the count.

Check out others who think we hit it out of the park at www.mlbjourney.com!

Celebrating the life of Della Marie Cochran, Dayna's mom and loving Nan Nan to Jack and Grant. We know you were with us during this whole journey. We miss hugging you after Pirates games, and eating warm cookies you made with love as you listened to our stories about the day at the ballpark. You were our biggest fan, and taught us to dream.

Contents

FOREWORD
by Bud Black

I have been involved in MLB for over thirty years as a player, manager, and coach, and I have been a sports fan for as long as I can remember. When I was growing up in southwest Washington State, we all played the sport that fit the season; football in the fall, basketball in the winter, and baseball in the spring and summer. There was never a time when baseball wasn't my favorite, and I remember eagerly waiting for the cold and rain to give way to spring, when I could finally pull out my glove and bat and head to the diamond. It wasn't so different than what I do these days, now that I think about it.

My father and uncle had a profound impact on my love of baseball, as they were always huge fans and made sure my childhood was peppered with baseball traditions. My father's favorite team was the San Francisco Giants, and in the time-honored tradition of these things, that became my favorite team as well. Willie Mays was our hero, of course. I remember pressing an old radio to my ear as a kid, where I could faintly catch the Giants' games being broadcast on KNBR, and listening to him make history throughout the 1960s.

My uncle was a Los Angeles Dodgers fan, and thought the world of their pitcher, Sandy Koufax. I remember him telling me throughout my childhood that he wanted me "to pitch like Sandy." It took me many years to realize that no one could pitch quite like Sandy! Many of you will know that the Giants and the Dodgers have one of the fiercest rivalries in baseball, dating back to their days as clubs based in New York City around the turn of the century. You have to remember that back then, there were no Seattle Mariners, and it was just a matter of time before I got scooped up into the amazing world of California baseball, where I find myself today. I pitched in the major leagues for many years, and am honored to have become friends with Sandy, so I figure I have gotten about as close as I could!

I first officially met the Haferkamps during spring training at Talking Stick, the Diamondbacks' and Rockies' facility, in 2011. I remember being struck right away by their genuine, visible enthusiasm for the game. The smiles on their faces and the energy they carried with them (even in the parking lot of the ballpark!) were easy to see. They were respectful, outgoing, and friendly right from the beginning.

After meeting them in Arizona, I got to know them better back in San Diego, where we were dedicated to the San Diego Padres, myself as manager and they as fans. As the years went on, we got to know each other better and better. The Haferkamp boys, Jack and Grant, in their amazing wigs were the talk of the dugout on more than one occasion. I remember picking them out of the crowd by those wigs and their homemade signs when the Padres were on the road all over North America.

The Haferkamps have become easily recognizable at Peoria, the Padres' spring training facility, and elsewhere in the Cactus League, where we hold spring training every March. It was always great watching the boys scamper around for autographs, and being involved in the backfield, watching batting practice, and interacting with the players. They have become known by many as truly dedicated Padres fans. Deep down, though, they are genuine fans of the game itself, and of all the teams, both major and minor.

I remember one exhibition game a few years ago, when we (the Padres) were playing the Cincinnati Reds at Goodyear Park. As the game was starting, I looked up into the stands and saw Steve, not in Padres gear, but in Reds gear! And Grant was a bat boy for the Reds, on top of that. As we made eye contact, I lifted my arms as if to say, "What's going on?" It was definitely funny, and Steve told me later he felt a bit sheepish about it. I forgave him, of course! The whole event hammered home the fact that even though they might cheer for one team or another, the Haferkamps are ultimately *baseball* fans of the best and truest type. No matter who is playing or what the outcome is, being able to see the game with family is what it's all about.

Players, coaches, managers, and support staff are professionals who work very hard at their jobs. At the same time, however, we are entertainers, dedicated to putting on the best performance we can. There is no doubt that baseball is as much about the fans as it is about the players. The fans are there to see the players, and the players need the fans in more ways than one. I firmly believe that the majority of the players understand this connection.

What would our game be without the roar of the crowd, or the loyalty that leads to rivalries? I am confident when I say that this sport needs people like the Haferkamps to keep doing what they are doing, and to get other people excited. We need fans. We need kids to play. Just like my father and uncle helped me fall in love with our great game, Steve and Dayna have passed on their passion to Jack and Grant. In time the current generation will itself pass on the wonderful baseball traditions that have meant so much to us.

When the Haferkamps asked me to write this foreword, I was humbled. Their dedication to baseball and each other has carried them thousands of miles, to dozens of ballparks, and this book will give you a peek into the fantastic experiences they had. I have been a player, a manager, and more, and I can say that you would be hard pressed to find better ambassadors for both the game of baseball and family values than Steve, Dayna, Jack, and Grant. This family is really doing its part to preserve the long legacy we have of enjoying the national pastime. I hope that as you read their story, you are inspired to check out for yourself all the wonderful things these ballparks, and our beautiful game, have to offer!

The Play Ball Kid

The baseball journey of a lifetime, how did it all begin? Thirty stadiums in five years certainly seems like a lot! It did take a while, but it was carefully planned, and our hope is to inspire you to believe in this dream of watching America's favorite pastime across the United States and Canada with family and friends. This is a story about a good, old-fashioned road trip, even though we traveled on planes, trains, and automobiles, and even a few horses, golf carts, and bicycles! In the end we hit 'em all, and had a ball!

Sports have always been an important part of our lives. Dayna grew up near Pittsburgh, a city where being a sports fan is in the blood, and it seems like everyone is always buzzing over the latest result, trade, or draft for the local teams. She attended baseball games with her father in the 70s, and has always had fond memories of the smells and sounds of stadiums, and the thrill of the game itself. Watching baseball on television was an almost nightly tradition in her childhood home, as her father enjoyed watching the Pirates after his workday at the family business.

Steve grew up in a quiet town in Florida named Jupiter. Like most small towns, Jupiter had a local hero: Bob Shaw. Shaw played in the major leagues from 1957 to 1967, and became good friends with Steve's parents when they moved to Jupiter in 1972. Shaw had been a pitcher, and had famously faced down opposing pitcher and Hall of Famer Sandy Koufax during the 1959 World Series. Although Steve preferred football and fishing with his older brother Clay in the Loxahatchee River when young, he was always a sports fan, and would occasionally catch a game at the West Palm Beach Stadium, home to the minor league West Palm Beach Expos. However, it was Shaw who would end up getting Steve more interested in baseball when he appeared at a youth league opening day in Jupiter dressed in his full World Series attire. This image, and the baseball history Jupiter had, would end up making Steve a fan of baseball for life. Even though it seemed like, at the time, baseball wasn't a big deal in Jupiter, it definitely was. While love of the major league ballgame experience had been a part of Dayna's life since the beginning, it was always right around the corner from Steve as well! There were a few other highly regarded Jupiter citizens associated with the area American Legion team who would go on to have great futures in baseball; Kevin O'Sullivan and Dante Bichette. O'Sullivan is head coach of the Florida Gators baseball team, and three-time College World Series coach. He actually grew up right down the street from Steve. Bichette would go on to play major league ball and be a four-time All-Star.

Anyway, we met in Denver, another sports-loving town, and got married shortly after, not realizing at the time what a big part of our lives baseball would become! We eventually settled in Carlsbad, California, in the beautiful La Costa Valley. We are both very active people, and have always been sports fans. Once our sons, Jack and Grant, were born, it was only natural to want to include them in these family traditions. In fact, in Jack's case, baseball has been a factor since the very beginning!

The day Jack was born, we were preparing for his arrival at Scripps Memorial Hospital in La Jolla, California. A baseball game was on even then, and the local San Diego Padres were facing off against the Cincinnati Reds. Despite Dayna being in labor, Steve and Dr. Harkey were glued to the television screen, commenting on each play and laughing as though they were at a sports bar rather than a hospital. Soon enough, the big moment came, and they were pried away from the game. At the exact moment that Jack was born, Mark Loretta hit a double to left field for the Padres. Everyone, including the at-the-time youngest baseball fan in the world, was cheering! After getting settled, we finished watching the game and opened a bottle of champagne. Our friend Lea brought Grant shortly after, who got to meet his little brother for the first time. Big Brother had a special gift for his little brother. Can you guess what it was? The world's smallest baseball glove!

We quickly found, as the boys grew, that baseball games stood out as the most family-friendly option when it came to attending live, professional sporting events. It is almost always a relaxed, friendly environment, and fit the bill for the sort of experience we wanted for the boys. The pace of the game allows for breaks to chat with friends, time to go and grab a snack, or just to stretch your legs and enjoy the view. Some sports, on the other hand, tend to be intense and often stressful when seen live. Professional football games, for example, tend to attract a more adult crowd, and sometimes you have to be careful where you sit! On top of all that, the much longer season length (for baseball) meant that ticket prices were often more affordable for a family of four.

Of course, it helped that our sons had always loved baseball in particular. They loved playing it, watching it, and talking about it. In fact, Dayna even let them play in the house from time to time...that is, until Grant hit a line drive right through the window! They loved hearing stories about famous players, and recounting their own exploits to one another in order to recreate the excitement and thrill of the game. They even learned their alphabets from a baseball themed book! Steve started coaching when Grant was very little and getting ready for the "big leagues" by playing t-ball. The youth baseball Pony League he coaches in is the La Costa Youth Organization (LCYO), which is a healthy combination of competition and fun. It offers a good mix, since while everyone wants to have a great time, they all, including the kids, want to improve at the game and play well. Even when we were watching television, baseball was always a safe, easy, and fun option when the boys were around. All we had to do was flip on a game, and soon the whole family would be entranced! Eventually, baseball became our family's primary pastime.

It didn't hurt that our home stadium, Petco Park, home of the San Diego Padres, was one of the newest, most beautiful, and most child-friendly baseball fields in the MLB. Even though it was designed and built during the heyday of retro-inspired stadiums, the heavy red brick of the Northeast tradition would not have fit into San Diego's warm, beachy, Californian vibe. The designers decided to go in a different direction. The ballpark pays tribute to its location with a beautiful sandstone and stucco exterior and ocean-blue seats, and a ship's whistle is played every time the Padres hit a home run at the park. The park's concourses are open on all sides, so fans can appreciate the great views of the city, the San Diego Bay, and the game at the same time. The Padres moved to Petco in 2004 from the multi-use Qualcomm Stadium, and we starting attending games as a family there soon afterwards.

Petco Park has also worked diligently to maintain a sense of history, and its designers and management have gone to great lengths to preserve some features of local interest. One of these is the famous Western Metal Supply Co. Building. Built in 1909, this four-story red brick building was originally used for the storage and distribution of engine parts, roofing material, and all manner of other metal supply needs, primarily in steel. The business supplied San Diego for several decades, but overall economic repression in the area hit the company hard in the 1960s. By the 1970s, the Western Metal Supply Co., along with a number of other companies in the industrial area, had gone bankrupt.

The building had been designed by the famous Chicago architect Henry Lord Gay. This detail, coupled with the age of the building, prompted the City of San Diego in the early 1980s to place the Western Metal Supply Co. Building on the list of historic sites in the city. This later encouraged the architects of Petco Park, itself completed in 2004, to incorporate the building into their designs, completely renovate it, and reinforce its foundation to be more earthquake resistant. Petco Park was built around this historic site, and now a particularly well-hit foul ball deep past left field might hit it directly! In past years, it was one of our favorite places to catch a game. We would buy regular tickets to get into the stadium, and then go up to the top of the building and walk through the Padres' Hall of Fame. There was a big carving station and a nice bar on the fourth floor that we would enjoy before getting in line to go out on the patio and watch the game for a few innings. It was a wonderful view and a great way to enjoy the game.

Another great feature that makes attending Petco unique is the Park at the Park. This is a grassy area attached to the stadium that contains a miniature baseball field for kids, a large monitor for watching the game, plenty of space for picnics, and a great view of the main field at the top of the hill. It is an ideal setup for families, and is budget-friendly, since you can bring your own food and tickets are offered at a significantly reduced price. Jack and Grant almost always end up making some plays at the mini-field, since the Park at the Park opens several hours before the opening pitch. If you want a good view of the field, however, stake your claim early at the top of the field, as this is a popular spot that fills quickly.

This was a fantastic early stadium for the boys to experience. Petco Park has a number of amenities that make it attractive, both to those with or without children. Stadium staff organized many fun activities, like face painting, for kids. In our earliest ballpark memories, the boys would come home with temporary tattoos and big smiles. When they were young we would always take advantage of those treats, and visit the Jr. Padre Booth, so the boys were all excited and involved in the trips to the stadiums.

The food at Petco is another great perk, as it has gotten very good over the years. Fish tacos, tri tip from the seaside market (affectionately known by locals as "Cardiff crack"), a fully stocked wine bar—there is something for everyone. There are also a hitting station and pitching machines, which are used in wonderful promotions held occasionally in the park. Fans of the game have the chance during the "Swing for Your Seats" event to swing at a single, high-speed pitch from the machine. If you get a home run, the reward is season tickets! In anticipation of hosting the 2016 All Star Games, the park installed a beautiful new high-definition Jumbotron, currently the largest in the National League and the third largest in Major League Baseball as a whole. We've taken the Petco Park Tour, and our guide gave us the scoop on the operations that take place in the press box on game days, inside the dugout, and the bullpen. Next to the Padre booth and pitching area is a small-scale replica of the USS Midway aircraft carrier. The hyper-realistic model is over ten feet long, and is a fascinating item to check out when you are in the neighborhood. San Diego has a long naval history, and we recommend checking out the museum. Getting to know our local stadium from every angle has made us all bigger fans of the game than ever, and we highly recommend scheduling these types of tours at Petco and any other ballpark!

We have seen some great moments at Petco, starting in 2006 when we saw Trevor Hoffman break the career save record. In 2009 we saw Scott Hairston hit a walk-off home run in the tenth inning in a win over the Mets. Interestingly enough, this was a record-breaking game, as it marked the first time in MLB history that a team had won four games in a row by a score of 2 to 1! The next morning, the boys joined in on the fitness workout the Pad Squad offers every Sunday with the Friar, the team mascot, played in the sand at the beach, and got some autographs before we headed to our seats. We were glad we had gotten to the stadium early after the opening pitch—this game was thrilling! Both teams scored plenty of runs on the way to an 8 to 6 victory for San Diego. Both teams scored three runs in the first inning, and then went back and forth until the eighth inning, when Tony Clark, first baseman, hit a three-run home run that would win the Padres the game. This was a pinch-hit home run. A pinch-hitter is a batter who replaces another batter on the roster at a critical point in the game; the idea is that a team might hang on to certain power hitters, then sub them in when they are needed to make a big play. This was the only season that switch-hitting Clark would play for the Padres. He played for many different teams over his long career, and we were thrilled to watch him play for San Diego for even a short time. After taking the lead, the Padres put in famed closer Trevor Hoffman, who would do what he was best at and stop the Mets dead in their tracks.

The next full weekend we spent at the ballpark as a family was in late May of 2009, and it was wonderful, incredibly eventful, and had wide-reaching ramifications for our lives! The Padres were facing off against the Chicago Cubs, and it was a great weekend to be a Padres fan! They had won seven games in a row, and fan excitement was high. A common sentiment at the time was that the move to Petco in 2004 had done great things for the team in general. In the first game, the Cubs took the lead in the second inning, but the Padres responded with two runs in the fourth inning and one in the seventh, and took the victory. The success of the Padres during this run was attributed to their strong lineup of pitchers, who had been holding opponents to very low scores. Grant was six and Jack was four, and they were both getting old enough to love every part of the ballpark experience. The boys had made up signs that said "Where's the Friar?" and "Padres are on fire!" and proudly joined in the celebrations, cheering their hearts out. They met Red Ruff and Blue Mew, mascots of Petco, and played baseball in the mini-park, and just had a wonderful time.

This game had a touch of history to it, as it marked the twenty-fifth anniversary of when the Padres had beaten the Cubs three games to two in the Nation League Championship. Before the game, members of the 1984 team met fans in the Park at the Park for a small celebration and autograph signing. Kurt Bevacqua, Dave Dravecky, Steve Garvey, Greg Harris, Terry Kennedy, Craig Lefferts, and more were in attendance, and all fans who attended received a special t-shirt commemorating that moment in Padres history. The lines were long, but dedicated fans walked away with signed cards, balls, placards, and more. After signing autographs, the players piled into white limousines and were driven onto the field. They were individually announced, their name and image broadcast on the Jumbotron, to the cheers of the crowd. It was a great moment, on a beautiful, sunny day. Padres 1984 NL Champions Weekend was an awesome experience!

We didn't think the weekend could possibly get any better, but we were wrong! We spent the night at the Marriott Gaslamp Hotel across the street, something that became a bit of a tradition of ours. We have always liked to make an exciting event of a ballgame, with a fun hotel stay beforehand, and the boys really love the Gaslamp. The staff at the hotel dress up in Padres jerseys on game days, and there is always plenty of old-fashioned candy like taffy, pixie sticks, and Necco wafers at the front desk for kids to grab before heading out to the game. We also recommend you take the elevator all the way up to the top, to the Altitude Sky Lounge, which has an incredible view. We got to the stadium early the next day, excited to see what the Padres had in store. In fact, we were first in line when the stadium opened, like we so often were!

Getting to the stadium early to beat the crowds ended up being an important wrinkle in the story of how we got started on our journey. It is a tradition of ours due to the consistent perks, like being able to watch the pitchers warm up, or catching a favorite player for an autograph before the game, but this day ended up surpassing all others. As the boys were playing on the mini-field before the game, we were approached by the Pad Squad leader, who asked if the boys would be interested in being the Play Ball kids for the day's game. It is a tradition, before many professional baseball games, for someone to holler "Play ball!" and get things going at the start of the first inning. The boys were thrilled and eagerly agreed, and for the first time we found out how rewarding it can be to be in the right place at the right time!

Before the opening pitch, as the television crews were readying for the opening ceremony, Jack and Grant were escorted out onto the field, where they were told that not only would they be starting off the game, they would be featured on the Jumbotron in front of the whole crowd. We weren't sure they could get more excited, but somehow, they managed! Grant described the feeling afterwards, saying that being in the field, seeing it stretch out in front of them, was awe-inspiring. Its massive size and the cheering fans made him feel like he had envisioned his dream of being a pro player. Being able to yell "Play ball!" is the dream of every little kid, and that excitement overcame the nervousness they both felt while walking the same turf as those great players.

At just the right moment, as the crowd bubbled with the excitement that precedes every game, Grant yelled "Play ball!" with all his might into the microphone, while Jack stood by his side and looked on with wide eyes. The crowd erupted into cheers, and the boys were escorted back to us, all smiles. As they were leaving the field, Ivan Dejesus, one of the Cubs' coaches, tossed them a ball from the Cubs' dugout and told them they had done a great job. We could tell as they walked over that they were proud and hooked for life!

The Padres extended their winning streak to nine games, as they blew out the Cubs by a score of 7 to 2. This entire winning streak took place at home, our own Petco! The game was exciting, both for its context and its content. There was a lot of action, as Kouzmanoff hit a three-run home run, and he and three other Padres hit doubles. Team spirit was very high. The third run was scored on an uncommon play, called a suicide squeeze. This play occurs when there is a runner on third base. The batter intends to bunt, and as soon as the pitch is released, the player on third takes off for home. The idea is that the batter is often gotten out at first base, "sacrificing" himself so that the player on third can score. In this game, the batter was David Eckstein, whose wife Ashley a year or so later would be responsible for the onset of the Star Wars craze at Petco, including the Yoda backpack in the Padres bullpen, which would also influence us!

We ate hot dogs and enjoyed the game immensely as a family, and headed out of the stadium after a perfect baseball weekend. On the way home and through the evening, the boys continued chattering about the day, the game, and the plays, both those made by the pros on the big field, and those made by themselves on the mini one.

The next morning at breakfast, Grant and Jack surprised us; they had apparently been whispering and plotting in their bunk beds well into the night. Grant said, "Jack and I have been thinking about an idea, and we think it would be fun to go to all thirty MLB stadiums as a family." Even at such a young age, they had paid enough attention to realize, and mention, that one of them was in Canada! They were also excited about commemorating the trip by getting small souvenirs or mementos at each stadium along the way.

It was too perfect of an idea to pass up. Of course, we loved the history and thrill of sports already, loved watching the competition and experiencing the culture of various games. Baseball was the most fam-ily-friendly, inexpensive, and fun, so it made sense. We had also been thinking of putting a concerted effort into organizing and executing more family activities just like this, and we knew that the memories we would create by taking this kind of journey would last forever. Although some folks that we told our plans to thought it was unusual that we wanted to make baseball, something that usually just the guys would do, a family event, we instantly knew it would work perfectly for us. So, we answered the boys excitedly—yes! When pestered further about the next stadium we would visit, Dayna smiled and said that of course it would be PNC Park, home to her own Pittsburgh Pirates.

From the very beginning of the trip, everyone in the family was excited. There was no real hesitation, even though we knew it would involve a lot of planning and careful budgeting. We knew that this was going to be something of a legacy for our family. Since the boys had initially brought up the idea, we involved them in the planning stages from the get-go. We tried to let them pick the next stadium on the trip. They loved discussing the ins and outs of each one, and going over the minutiae of their baseball trivia while hunting for the perfect next stadium. Once they had settled on where to go next, we would build up a trip around the area and begin to consider hotels, museums, restaurants, and local sights. Involving them from the beginning made the entire process more exciting, and made it feel like a real family effort! Before we get much farther, let us assure you that this is very doable, even if at first glance it seems financially or logistically daunting. If you decide this is something you would like to do with your family, just spread your trips out. It took us five summers to finish our tour of the stadiums, and the entire endeavor was easier broken up into smaller chunks. We encourage you to start planning now, and to make a wish list of the stadiums you may want to hit first.

We were, and still are, fans of other sports as well. Despite going with baseball as our primary family activity, we still avidly follow professional football. Choosing baseball as our family sport worked out in many ways, but one important one was that we didn't have to deal with feeling uncomfortable for rooting for different teams when we were visiting their stadiums! In football, we are diehard Pittsburgh Steelers fans, due in no small part to Dayna's influence. This kind of team loyalty didn't seem quite as important when it came to baseball, and during the process of picking stadiums, we never butted heads over team rivalries, because we admire and respect them all. While Steve will tend to root for the Padres, Grant the Reds, and Jack the Athletics, at the end of the day we like all the teams. Part of the tradition that we made up as we went along our journey with the national pastime is to root, root, root for the home team, and more often than not, we cheered loudest for them!

Mascots were an important feature of the ballpark experience for our family; even before the boys were old enough to truly appreciate the game. They loved seeing the Friar! Every mascot we've interacted with and seen on our journey has been fun, but some mascots hold special places in the hearts of baseball fans. One that we really love is the Famous San Diego Chicken. He is very well known, and it is partially credited for raising the standards of all mascots, especially in the MLB. He has been around since the 1970s. He doesn't show up at every Padres game (and he doesn't *just* show up at Padres games—he's also been a celebrated television star, and makes appearances all over town!), but when he does, it is a big deal! In fact, Steve's dad had once hired the San Diego Chicken to surprise his mother for her birthday!

The Chicken is widely traveled, and has been in everything from commercials for Sony and McDonalds to professional wrestling and football events. We were very glad to be able to see such a dedicated mascot back on his home turf, and we cheered with the rest of the crowd as he rounded home plate and theatrically planted the flag between third and home, right in front of the visiting team dugout.

Some teams have numerous mascots. The Cincinnati Reds, for example, have four regular mascots! Other teams have their signature mascot, and then they have sort of auxiliary folks that are there for some backup cheering. The Pittsburgh Pirates have the Jolly Roger, with the

Pirate Parrot as his sidekick. Many teams also incorporate certain mascots only for special occasions. At Petco, the main mascot is the Swinging Friar, but then on Father's Day, they also have the Grandpa Friar. The variations on mascots, how they interact with the crowd, and their roles in the ballpark experience were a constant source of fascination for us on our journey, and made every stadium that much more unique!

Three MLB teams don't have an *official* mascot (the New York Yankees, the Los Angeles Angels of Anaheim, and the Los Angeles Dodgers), but some of the unofficial ones are just as celebrated. The Angels' Rally Monkey, for example, is really energizing, and everyone is super excited by his appearance. The Rally Monkey is a real capuchin monkey who appears in different filmed clips at the Angels' stadium. Even though the Angels don't have a traditional mascot, the monkey performs that role really well. At Angels' home games, they start playing the song "Jump Around," and then the Rally Monkey appears on the Jumbotron to bounce around and encourage the home team to rally. Trust us, it's very contagious, and you can't help but jump around. He is definitely one of our favorites, so of course, we bought the Rally Monkey doll! Mascots who interact well with the crowd can get everyone pumped, even people who aren't the world's biggest baseball fans! We took our little Rally Monkey to the opening day game with the Texas Rangers. We were in the outfield with our age-old gear on, and we hung the Rally Monkey up there. An Angel coach, who caught the fly ball in batting practice, threw it to us because we had the Rally Monkey and he noticed it out of the corner of his eye.

Mascot identification, especially on the road, shows a strong tie with the teams that can help you build relationships. Buying team souvenirs and then taking them to away games helps you to separate from the crowd, and can help you get autographs or attention. It's why the Angels' coach gave us the ball; there were other Angels' fans there, but our boys had the monkey. When he looked up and saw that, he smiled, and threw the ball up to us. It was an instant connection with him, and hopefully it helped brighten his day as much as he brightened ours.

The Mascot Hall of Fame covers all sorts of sports teams and other activities, and has three members from Major League Baseball—the Philly Phanatic, Mr. Met, and the Cleveland Indians' Slider. Fans and teams take their mascots very seriously, and we highly recommend you spend the time to get to know the mascot before you visit a stadium—it will enhance your experience in so many ways! As you start your own baseball stadium journey, we've provided a handy cheat sheet to mascot identification for you.

TEAM	Mascot	More Info
Arizona Diamondbacks	D. Baxter the Bobcat, The Luchador	D. Baxter is a bobcat in a Diamondbacks uniform. He was inspired by a mashup of "D-Backs" and their stadium's old name, "Bank One Ballpark," or BOB. The Luchador, a man in a lucha libre wrestling mask and a Diamondbacks uniform, was introduced in 2013 as a second mascot.
Atlanta Braves	Homer the Brave	Homer is a baseball head in an Atlanta Braves uniform. He replaced "Chief Noc-a-Homa," a controversial Native American caricature, in 1989.
Baltimore Orioles	The Oriole Bird	The Bird is an oriole, the state bird of Maryland, in a baseball cap.
Boston Red Sox	Wally the Green Monster	Wally is a large muppet-looking character introduced in 1997. His name alludes to Fenway Park's famous Green Monster, the large wall in the park's left field.
Chicago Cubs	Clark	Introduced in 2014, Clark is a furry bear cub named after one of Wrigley Field's address cross streets.
Chicago White Sox	Southpaw	Southpaw is a green muppet-looking character with yellow fur and a White Sox uniform.
Cincinnati Reds	Mr. Red, Gapper, Mr. Redlegs, Rosie Red	Mr. Red, the original mascot, is a giant baseball head.
		Gapper is a large red furry creature, introduced when the team moved into the Great American Ballpark.
		Mr. Redlegs is a retro-styled, mustachioed baseball head.
		Rosie Red is a female baseball head.

Cleveland Indians	Slider	Slider is a fuzzy purple and yellow character introduced in 1990. Slider is a member of the Mascot Hall of Fame.
Colorado Rockies	Dinger	Dinger is a purple triceratops, chosen after the Rockies unearthed dinosaur bones during stadium construction.
Detroit Tigers	Paws	Paws is a tiger in a baseball uniform.
Houston Astros	Orbit	Orbit is a green, furry alien character with antennae and an Astros uniform, celebrating Houston's history as "Space City," the home of NASA's manned flight center.
Kansas City Royals	Sluggerrr	Sluggerrr is a lion in a Royals uniform with a stylized mane that looks like a crown. He's best known for shooting hot dogs into the stands.
Miami Marlins	Billy the Marlin	Billy is a marlin with arms and legs introduced when the team was created in 1993. The marlin is a type of billfish, hence the name "Billy."
Milwaukee Brewers	Bernie Brewer	Bernie is a plush cartoon man with a large yellow mustache created to honor Milt Mason, a dedicated fan.
Minnesota Twins	T.C. Bear	A bear in a Twins uniform introduced in 2000, T.C. Bear pays homage to the Hamm's Beer Bear. The "T.C." in his name comes from the Twin Cities moniker for Minneapolis and St. Paul.
New York Mets	Mr. and Mrs. Met	A baseball head in a Mets uniform, Mr. Met was the league's first official mascot (1964). His baseball head partner, Mrs. Met, was introduced in 1975. Mr. Met is a member of the Mascot Hall of Fame.
Oakland Athletics	Stomper	A large elephant in an A's uniform, this mascot pays homage to the team's early days as the Philadelphia Athletics. As the story goes, the team was referred to by a rival team as a "white elephant" for its owners, and the nickname stuck.

Philadelphia Phillies	Phillie Phanatic	A member of the Mascot Hall of Fame, this shaggy green character has a large snout and wears a Phillies uniform. He was introduced in 1978.
Pittsburgh Pirates	Pirate Parrot	A large green parrot, this mascot was introduced in 1979. He is also well known for shooting hot dogs into the crowd.
San Diego Padres	Swinging Friar	A cartoon friar complete with traditional habit, the Swinging Friar has been associated with the team since its early days in the Pacific Coast Leagues.
San Francisco Giants	Lou Seal	A giant grey seal wearing a Giants uniform, this mascot's full name is Luigi Francisco Seal. He was introduced/ born on July 25, 1996. Legend has it that former manager Dusty Baker first discovered the seal on pier 39.
Seattle Mariners	Mariner Moose	He's a giant moose in a Mariners uniform.
St. Louis Cardinals	Fredbird	An anthropomorphic cardinal in the team's uniform, this mascot's name is a play on the cardinal's "redbird" moniker. He is best known for "beaking" the heads of fans.
Tampa Bay Rays	Raymond	A furry "Seadog" with long blue hair, Raymond wears oversized shoes and a backwards baseball cap. The team claims he was discovered by fishermen in the Gulf of Mexico.
Texas Rangers	Rangers Captain	An anthropomorphic horse, the Rangers Captain wears number 72 on his uniform to commemorate the Rangers move to their current location in 1972.
Toronto Blue Jays	Ace	Ace, baseball slang for a great pitcher, is a blue jay in large white shoes.
Washington Nationals	Screech	A bald eagle (the national bird) wearing a Nationals uniform, Screech was "hatched" in 2005.

Along with mascots, the songs and musical traditions of each ball-park definitely sparked our curiosity from the beginning of our journey. As we continued along and visited them all, we noticed that many teams had special songs and sometimes even dance routines that they employed throughout the game. The seventh-inning stretch, for example, is a long-standing tradition in baseball with a highly disputed history, but it definitely stems from a time when fans were watching from far less comfortable seats. During the seventh-inning stretch, everyone at the ballgame takes a few minutes to stand up, walk about, and sing some great songs together. Every stadium we visited played the classic "Take Me Out to the Ball Game," and many also played "God Bless America" for games on Sundays. This latter song was added after 9/11, and has turned into another welcome tradition. A lot of teams also add in a fun sing-along song too, and watching the hometown fans really get into it inspired us to learn a few of our own to join in the fun! Here's a list of some of our favorites we encountered along the way, seventh-inning stretch or otherwise!

Stadium	Team	Stadium Songs!
Angel Stadium of Anaheim	Angels	"Build Me Up Buttercup" The Foundations
AT&T Park	Giants	"Bye Bye Baby" –Bay City Rollers
Busch Stadium	Cardinals	"Meet Me in St. Louis, Louis" Instrumental, "Here Comes the King"
Citi Field	Mets	"Lazy Mary" Lou Monte, "Piano Man" Billy Joel
Comerica Park	Tigers	"Don't Stop Believin'" Journey
Coors Field	Rockies	Cover version of "Hey! Baby," originally by Bruce Channel
Dodger Stadium	Dodgers	"I Love LA" Randy Newman

Fenway Park	Red Sox	"Sweet Caroline" Neil Diamond
Globe Life Park	Rangers	"Cotton-Eyed Joe" Instrumental
Great American Ball Park	Reds	"Cincinnati Ohio" Connie Smith
Kauffman Stadium	Royals	"Friends in Low Places" Garth Brooks
Marlins Park	Marlins	"Louie Louie" The Kingsmen
Miller Park	Brewers	"The Beer Barrel Polka"
Minute Maid Park	Astros	"Deep in the Heart of Texas"
Nationals Park	Nationals	"Take on Me" A-ha
Oakland Coliseum	Athletics	"2 Legit 2 Quit" MC Hammer
Oriole Park at Camden Yards	Orioles	"Thank God I'm a Country Boy" John Denver
Petco Park	Padres	"You've Lost That Lovin' Feelin'" The Righteous Brothers
Progressive Field	Indians	"Hang on Sloopy" The McCoys
Rogers Centre	Blue Jays	"OK Blue Jays"
Turner Field	Braves	"The Tomahawk Chop" band song.
Wrigley Field	Cubs	"Take Me Out to the Ball Game" led by a different guest singer every game in memory of late announcer Harry Caray
Yankee Stadium	Yankees	"God Bless America" "Cotton Eyed Joe"

Sure, you can listen to these songs at any time, but nothing beats the experience of singing them at the top of your lungs with tens of thousands of other fans! It is very interesting to see what traditions have evolved around each of these songs at each field. At Rogers Centre, fans literally do callisthenic stretches in concert during "OK Blue Jays." At Progressive Field, fans spell out O-H-I-O at appropriate and synchronized times. During both "The Star Spangled Banner" in the beginning of the game and "Thank God I'm a Country Boy" at Camden Yards, Orioles (or "O's") fans belt out and hold their "O"s much longer! Learning these traditions and getting into the spirit of each stadium takes each ballpark to a new level, and teaches you so much about the individual and unique cultures of each—plus it's just plain fun!

As the kids get older, it's wonderful to see how much wisdom and confidence this journey has given them. Walking into another game at Petco Park in 2013, it was amazing how they just seemed like old hands. We had been given excellent seats by our friend Erik, a friend who coaches youth baseball and works for the Padres. The kids had crazy wigs on, and said hello to Bud Black, the Padres' coach, on their way in. We sat down and watched a great game of baseball against the Arizona Diamondbacks. It ended up being an important win for the home team. The past two seasons had been rough for the Padres, and they had had losing records for both. The game was looking bad initially, as the Diamondbacks got off to an early two-run lead after Miguel Montero hit a home run in the first inning. The Padres rallied, and Yasmani Grandal, switch-hitting catcher, hit a three-run homer in the fifth inning. The Padres wound up winning the game 6 to 4, and for the first time since early in the 2011 season, had a .500 record— thirty-four wins and thirty-four losses.

We saw a friend on the Jumbotron, and then we were featured on the Jumbotron in the seventh inning, where another friend (the boys' teacher) saw us! She came over to watch the Saturday night fireworks with us. After the game, Kyle Blanks gave Grant his home run bat. We ended the evening laughing and talking about the excitement over gummy bears and ice cream in a room at the Residence Inn. As our boys fell asleep, we watched over them proudly. No longer little kids, they carry themselves with dignity, and they have made meaningful connections and built fantastic relationships with people at stadiums throughout MLB. They have learned so much about baseball, how to take an experience from good to great, and making the most out of a special time from this trip. Every moment has been worth it, building these fantastic memories, and we can't wait to share our tips, tricks, advice, and stories with you, so that you can take your own stadium journey!

CHAPTER TWO
We are Family

Saying that Pittsburgh is a big sports town is an understatement. Along with the Pirates, Pittsburgh is home to the Steelers football team (six-time Super Bowl champions) and Penguins hockey team (three-time Stanley Cup champions). All three Pittsburgh teams wear black and gold, and have long histories and dedicated fan bases in the city and beyond. The 1970s were a great time to be a Pittsburgh fan, as both the Steelers and the Pirates were wildly successful. The Steelers won four Super Bowls in that time, and the Pirates won the World Series in 1971 and 1979. Dayna's father (Pap Pap to the boys) had season tickets to the Steelers for the family back then, and they attended games for both teams.

The Pirates have a fascinating history, and their formation was integral to the development of professional baseball. In the 1870s, there were several semi-professional baseball teams playing in various towns and cities on the area of the Allegheny River that runs through modern Pittsburgh. There were also several competing leagues at the time, foremost among them the National League, Players League, and American Association. One of these teams, based on where its various home fields were located, was known as the Alleghenys. In 1887 this team transferred from the AA to the NL, which was a severe blow to the former organization. In similar fashion, in 1890 many of the Alleghenys left the team to play for the Burghers, another Pittsburgh team, but with the PL. After some clever paperwork and restructuring, the team was able to scoop up its players again, and sign a star second baseman, Lou Bierbauer, from the Philadelphia Athletics. At the time Bierbauer wasn't officially on the Athletics' roster, but they took the Allegheny managers' action poorly and decried the "piratical" nature of the move! The name stuck, and by 1912, the Pittsburgh Pirates were playing in Pittsburgh to stay. Arrrgh!

Pittsburgh was also home to three teams in the Negro Leagues: the Pittsburgh Keystones, the Homestead Grays, and the Pittsburgh Crawfords. The Grays won twelve league titles, and the Crawfords won four consecutive league titles. They had many wonderful athletes, and Pittsburgh took pride in their accomplishments. The Pirates were one of the first baseball teams to make a stand for civil rights, petitioning for the integration of MLB starting in the 1940s, and they continued to push boundaries and challenge the status quo well into the 1970s.

The championship teams of the 1970s were helmed by many notable players, including Baseball Hall of Famers Roberto Clemente and Willie Stargell. Willie was the one who suggested "We Are Family" by Sister Sledge as the theme song for the winning 1979 season, and it was a sensation that Dayna and her family remember well! It was all over Pittsburgh that summer, playing on the radio, on t-shirts, and stenciled on the dugout. When the Pirates won the World Series against the Orioles, the baseball players' wives jumped on top of the dugout to dance to the song, the precursor to many dances we saw performed at MLB stadiums on our journey.

As a team with a long tradition, the Pirates have played in many stadiums over the years. Three of the most notable are Forbes Field, Three Rivers Stadium, and the current PNC Park. The Pirates played at Forbes Field from 1909 to 1970. They won three World Series titles at the park. Forbes is still widely mourned as one of the most unusual and best baseball parks in MLB history, with a large playing area and many quirks that made it a very interesting field to both play on and watch games from.

Their next field, Three Rivers Stadium, was a doughnut multi-use stadium the team shared with the Steelers from 1970 until 2000. While the field boasted a beautiful location, and a lot of notable and amazing baseball was played there including the first World Series game played at night in 1971, there wasn't much else to recommend about it. When it was decided that it was time for the team to have a new field, the designers looked back to Forbes and the history of the team and the city for inspiration.

When PNC Park opened in 2001, everyone agreed they had knocked it out of the park, and it's remained a top-ranked stadium ever since. Following the retro renaissance of ballparks like Orioles Park in Camden Yards (which was largely inspired by the memory of Forbes field), PNC pays homage to the classic fields of baseball. It is one of the smaller parks, with around 38,000 seats arranged in two tiers, like the two oldest fields still in play, Wrigley and Fenway. Baseball is a sport best seen as close to the action as possible, and every seat at PNC provides an up-close view of the game. The highest seat is only eighty-eight feet away from the field! The main concourse is open, so you never have to miss a moment of the game.

The outfield is asymmetrical, like the classic fields, and there are other quirks, like a sharp corner in deep center field and a twenty-one foot right field wall with the Allegheny River running behind it, that makes both playing the field and watching the game quite exciting. The river is, in fact, less than 450 feet from home plate, and if you're lucky, you might witness a home run splash! Fans can arrive by riverboat, and line the banks on game days, tailgating, listening to live music on the riverfront stage, and hoping for stray balls. Clipper boats toot their horns as they pass by, delighting fans and adding to the ambiance.

You never forget you're in Pittsburgh while you're watching a game at PNC—it has a very unique design aesthetic. Unlike many of the neoclassical stadiums, PNC is built from limestone to complement the warm stone used extensively downtown, and exposed blue steel to honor Pittsburgh's steelmaking history. The center field's batter's eye is all landscaped in plants native to Pennsylvania—mountain laurels, Pennsylvania pines, and rhododendrons. There's an amazing view of downtown Pittsburgh over the bright yellow Roberto Clemente Bridge, which is closed to vehicles on game days so fans can park on the other side and walk over to the stadium—it's become quite a local tradition, and very special way to experience this ballpark.

Along with celebrating the history of the town and the team in usable ways in the stadium, like building the twenty-one-foot wall to honor Clemente's number, naming the main level food court Pop's Plaza after Willie "Pop" Stargell, and naming a nearby street Mazeroski Way to honor his induction to the Hall of Fame, the stadium experience includes many traditional historical mementos like statues and memorials.

A display of eighteen bats dedicated to members of the local Negro National Leagues teams can be found over the left field entrance. Banners celebrating former star players line the street sides of the park. Historic uniforms, photos, bats, baseball cards, retired numbers, and memorabilia can be found lining concourses and lounges. A statue of Honus Wagner has travelled from Forbes Field, to Three Rivers, and now has a home at PNC near the home plate entrance. Stargell's statue was dedicated on the day he passed away in 2001.

Three Rivers Stadium and Forbes Field are immortalized in the statue dedicated to Roberto Clemente, who played in both of them as the outfielder for the Pirates from 1955 to 1972. In the statue's base, dirt from these two stadiums can be found, as well as dirt from the first park Clemente played at, Santurce Field in Puerto Rico. This statue has always stood out to our family as a touching tribute to the history of the Pirates, one of its greatest players, and the power of friendship.

Roberto Clemente and Manny Sanguillén were teammates during the 60s and 70s, and were known as very close friends. Both were All-Stars, and won the World Series together in 1971. Clemente spent much of his time not only on the field but organizing the delivery of food, medication, and other goods throughout Latin America and the Caribbean. In 1972, he organized a series of planes packed with aid materials, to be sent to victims of an earthquake in Nicaragua. These planes never reached their destination, and Clemente began packing another one, that he planned on accompanying. The plane suffered a series of malfunctions and crashed off the coast of Puerto Rico. There were no survivors, and Clemente's brilliant career was cut short while in the service of others. After hearing of the crash, Manny rushed to the region to personally search for his friend. Their example to the rest of us, of friendship and excellence in competition, made visiting Clemente's statue a very worthwhile experience for our family. Being able to meet Manny, who can be found at a delicious BBQ stand (Manny's BBQ) within the stadium that bears his name, on the same day is a great reminder of exactly what this journey is all about for us.

Pap Pap had the opportunity to meet Roberto briefly in the late 1960s, and he will always remember the moment with a mixture of awe and incredulity. It was supposed to be at a scheduled autograph signing before the game in right field at Forbes Field. He and Deanna, Dayna's sister, had tried to make it in time but were running late, and missed the whole session! Pap Pap was devastated, and kept on apologizing as they wound their way through the stadium on their way to their seats. Suddenly, as they took a quick turn to grab some lunch, Clemente himself rounded a corner right in front of them! He was very kind, and stayed for a few minutes to speak with them. They both find it hard to believe, to this day, that it happened. This just goes to show you that you never know what is going to happen at the park, and being in the right place at the right time can certainly offer great surprises!

Family was the most important part of our trip. We love baseball, but it was always about family first. Dayna's mother passed in 2011, and continuing on this journey was a way to honor her tradition of sharing special moments with those closest to us. She believed that family was the most important thing, and it was a priority in her life. We wanted to further her legacy on this trip by reaching out to our family and sharing wonderful experiences with them.

Like we mentioned, Dayna is originally from a small town outside Pittsburgh, and she comes from a large family—she has five siblings: Dean, Deanna, Donell, Dixie, and Donnie. Dayna is the youngest, so some of her older siblings were really into baseball before she was. They were eagerly watching the 1971 Pirates' season, when they won the World Series. Dixie had a favorite player by the name of Bobby Robertson, who played first base. Deanna's favorite player was Richie Hebner, third baseman. These two sisters would bicker and banter back and forth over who had the better favorite player. They smile when they think back to that 1971 series, when Hebner and Robertson hit three-run homers in back-to-back games on their way to defeating the Orioles! Dayna and Donnie, one of her older brothers, would play pick-up baseball at a large field across the street from her childhood home even after the sun went down. Baseball was everywhere!

Well, now these close-knit siblings have spouses and children of their own, and the count is over twenty people! Since she grew up around and worked in Pittsburgh for so long, we have many relatives, coworkers, and friends in the area. Her company of over twenty-seven years, Federated Investors, can be seen from PNC Park in the gorgeous city skyline, a beautiful sight when sitting behind home plate! With so many extended family members still located in the Pittsburgh area, we have seen many games at PNC. Several of them have featured giveaways, and we have gotten stuffed pillows and helmets. We have also been able to include the most people for these games. We try to get together our biggest groups to root for the Pirates, and it isn't uncommon for us to pack up a dozen or more family and friends and take over a long stretch of seating. We can't mention PNC without also mentioning the delicious food, with Mrs. T's pierogies and Primanti Brothers' huge sandwiches stacked with coleslaw and French fries topping the charts! These local bites are definitely fan favorites, and have earned PNC Park a reputation for being one of the tastiest stadiums in MLB. This park has become something of a family stadium for us, our baseball home away from Petco.

Our decision to incorporate lots of family into a quest to visit all the MLB ballparks afforded some interesting opportunities. One of these took place when we went to see the Padres and Pirates play at PNC Park in 2008. As you might imagine, this was a special game already, since it was our current home team against Dayna's childhood home team. We ended up having a very large group of people who committed to coming. As the number of guests grew (eventually reaching twenty-two people!), we began thinking about a fun and effective way to get everyone to the stadium. As it happened, we were good friends with a bus driver for the local school system, and Dean was able to get a loan on one of the school buses! This was definitely a unique method of travel for most of those going, and provided entertainment all on its own. While our family friend Ron wasn't allowed to accept payment for his services, he was more than happy to accept our invitation to enjoy the game.

This particular trip ended up being very eventful. We were honored to get to meet Manny Sanguillén himself. Jack, who was celebrating his third birthday, made yet another appearance on the Jumbotron, this time on Dayna's shoulders. Pap Pap was our second birthday celebrant!

We attended the game as a mix of Padres and Pirates fans. It was a good day to be rooting for the Padres! Under the excellent management of Bud Black, Padres pitcher Jake Peavy pitched and batted a superb game. He struck out ten Pirates, and hit what would end up being a game-winning home run. It was a perfect day for baseball: bright, sunny, and clear.

This happened to be a good day for the Padres in Cooperstown as well, as "Goose" Gossage was inducted into the Hall of Fame. Gossage had pitched for both the Padres and the Pirates, and had begun a tradition of closing in San Diego that Trevor Hoffman would be a part of years later. Hoffman is a big deal for Padres fans, and we will be talking about him later!

There ended up being quite a few games over the course of our journey, especially at PNC Park, where we were able to organize groups of a dozen or more. Everything is better in that kind of crowd, even getting soaked by a squirt gun-toting, overly zealous home team mascot! In 2010, we were there for another clash of two of the Padres and the Pirates. We had just finished a tour of Heinz Field, the turf of the Pittsburgh Steelers, and were headed into PNC, when we saw that the players were heading into the park. We were able to find a spot in line before the players entered and got quite a few autographs.

After the tour and meeting the players, we settled into our seats. There were eighteen of us in attendance at that game, and the San Diego contingent was dutifully wearing its Padres attire. We love both teams, but had decided to go in our Padres gear, which earned us a squirt or two from the Pirate Parrot yet again, who wanders the crowd looking for targets. We got soaked! That ended up being just fine though, because although we were wet, the Padres played a great game and vindicated us.

The Padres were in high spirits: they were leading the NL West, had won three in a row, and had crushed the poor Pirates the day before 9 to 2. At first things seemed to be going well for the home club, as the Pirates gained an early two-run lead at the end of the first inning. It wasn't to last, however, as the Pirates struck back with five runs in the second. With a final score of 6 to 3, it wasn't the best day for the Pirates, who were in the middle of a rough season. Denorfia and Gonzalez hit home runs for San Diego, both of whom had signed balls for the boys before the game! We must have brought some luck with us from San Diego.

The boys were able to spend some time with Bud Black, the Padres manager. They also got autographs from a few other players in town (Luke Gregerson, pitcher; Mat Latos, pitcher). The whole crew had a wonderful time, and we were glad to be able to see another great game with our loved ones.

We celebrated the Fourth of July in 2012 with another large family trip to PNC Park to watch the Pirates take on the Astros. It was an extremely hot day, so we had decided to spring for club seats. Located on the second level, club seating offers a reprieve from the heat with an air-conditioned bar and restaurant area, video games, and pool tables. We had a patio area from which to watch the game, equipped with large, comfy seats. Despite these perks, Jack and Grant insisted, along with Uncle Dean, on staying out in our seats for most of the game, where they draped wet towels over their heads and carefully watched the game. We had ten other family members with us.

The game was pretty high scoring, and was a good one to see live. The Pirates were in the middle of one of the best seasons they had had in years, and fan excitement was riding high after a two-game winning streak. After a scoreless first inning, the Bucs came to life in the second, scoring three runs thanks in part to the efforts of local slugger Pedro

Álvarez. Two weeks earlier, Pedro had become the first Pirate to hit two home runs in back-to-back games in nearly one hundred years.

The Pirates were able to keep their lead, and despite a last inning comeback attempt by Houston, the game ended in Pittsburgh's favor, 6 to 4. We had a great day! PNC has been a great place for our family, and it is definitely one of the Haferkamps' favorite stadiums. Usually when we see games in Pittsburgh, we end up staying at the Springhill Suites North Shore, run by Marriott, which is also one of our favorite hotels. It is located right across the street from the park, and we highly recommend it.

Apart from our readymade cheering crew at PNC, we've really had a wonderful time meeting up with friends and family along the way and inviting people we care about to join us in games across the country. We've been able to explore Busch Stadium in St. Louis with local friends who met us at the ballpark to watch the game. We also got good seats and additional appreciation for the stadium from our friend John J. Smith, who was a long-time season ticket holder and who owns the masonry company that put in all the bricks at the stadium and ballpark village. Our trip to Yankee Stadium was made even better by meeting up with friends and enjoying the city. We included Steve's college friend, Alan, and his daughter Avery for what turned out to be a very special game at Turner Field, and it became quite a reunion—Steve ran into several other old fraternity friends from college, which was a great surprise! Dayna's sister and brother-in-law met up with us at Target Field for the Home Run Derby, and we also ran into friends there, and we love seeing our friends during local games at Petco.

We were able to experience both the Sun Life Stadium (now closed) and Marlins Park with Steve's parents. We convinced Pap Pap, Uncle Dean, and Aunt Doe to come to D.C. and join us at Nationals Park. We visited the Great American Ballpark with our Uncle Dean, who took the kids to their rainiest game ever, and the next night we met up with Steve's cousin Doug and his family. At U.S. Cellular Field, Steve's niece Katie came to meet up with us, along with her husband and their friends.

Over the course of visiting every MLB stadium, we found ourselves spending many wonderful hours with friends and family. Making a point from the beginning to always include the people that we love made our journey that much better, and we're so glad we were able to share these memories with them! We went to games with nephews and nieces, aunts and uncles, cousins, brothers, sisters, sisters-in-law, brothers-in-law, and friends—some of whom we hadn't seen in many years, and some that we all hadn't met as a family before! Over the course of our journey, we were able to experience nearly half of the stadiums in the company of loved ones. Certain games felt almost like family reunions, when we banded together in groups to invade the local ballpark.

Going to the games ended up being enjoyable even for those of our friends and family who weren't necessarily the biggest of baseball fans. Everyone who joined us at least liked baseball, but didn't necessarily love it. We found that inviting our loved ones along was just a great way to meet up and spend the day. Baseball is unique in professional sports that a lot of it is about just enjoying the time, and there's so much to do even if you're not highly focused on the game. One of the many perks of baseball as an event is that there are many other things to do and enjoy in conjunction with watching the game. Some stadiums have outstanding and interesting foods, for example, or dishes unique to a given area. For some people, family is the primary attraction. Our niece, Molly, has told us that while she has never gone to a baseball game by herself, she has gone to many with family and friends. Dayna's sister, Deanna, told us that she and her husband don't go to baseball games unless they know Jack and Grant will be there! There is something for everyone to enjoy, and sometimes meeting at a big venue for a particular event is the only chance some family members might have to see others. In that case you could do worse, and more expensively, than a ballgame!

As a family, we cheer most for the Pirates, the Padres, the Reds, the Oakland A's, and the Angels. But even at home, we really will watch any game that's on! Everyone we met up with along the way has different teams they like, which was one of the reasons why we would reach out to them when we were going to their city. Since, as a family, we frequently rooted for the home team when we were visiting their stadium, it was great to have hometown fans along with us to show us the traditions of their local teams! It really enhanced the experience and taught us so much. Baseball is a very idiosyncratic sport, and there are so many inside jokes and interesting pieces of history around each aspect; having people there with us who were excited to share information about their teams was always an education in itself.

It was also great to attend the games with people who were at different stages in their lives, to see what they brought out of the experience. We spent time with some people that were young, in their twenties, who didn't have children, and with grandparents who enjoyed reliving their childhood baseball memories with our boys. Everyone took something different out of the games, and we all had a great time!

We reached out to people that we met up with along the way and asked what they thought of the experience. We wanted to get their perspectives, since they were coming at it from different places in their lives. We knew why we were there—we wanted to hit 'em all, and create wonderful memories with our loved ones! We wanted to see why they enjoyed it, and how this type of adventure could be enjoyed by all sorts of different people. There are many happy memories associated with the trip, and the family and friends who accompanied us were gracious enough to give their thoughts on the trips. We've included some of them here, to give some perspective on how a wide range of people with a host of interests love being included, to hopefully inspire you to make the same connections when you start your journey!

Robert M., our nephew who was living in Kentucky and studying at the time to become a doctor, joined us for some Pittsburgh Pirates games.

I would always try and join up and attend a game when the whole family was getting together; it was always a good time to see everyone. Most people follow sports by season (i.e. football in the fall and basketball in the winter). The Haferkamps follow baseball from the draft and spring training all the way into the playoffs. This is exciting to see at a live game, since they know about a lot of players.

My favorite memory from attending these games with the family was when I was working on chemistry research, and I heard that they were going to a Pirates game in Pittsburgh. I had a couple days off coming up, and I decided to fly up spontaneously and surprise them. From this experience, I learned the value of down time and how baseball can relax anyone.

Doug C., Steve's cousin, a traveling nurse who lives in Ohio, brought his wife (also a nurse) and three kids to meet us for a Reds' game.

I was excited to see my family in my home city, and to be able to go to our ballpark for a great night of Reds' baseball. That's all the motivation I needed. It was fabulous!!

My favorite memory was experiencing Homer Bailey's no-hitter with all of us in attendance, and seeing the excitement build inning after inning, and being part of baseball's rare feat! I've been in and around baseball my whole life, and I guess what I've learned in this game is you are never to expect the expected. To see a no-hitter on any particular night is a rare and special feat indeed, and to experience one with your family...quite special indeed!! It was great being with all of you, especially the boys, in our home atmosphere, seeing a Reds' victory. As we say...this one belongs to the Reds!!!

Molly C., Dayna's niece, is an on-air broadcaster for Accuweather who lives in State College, Pennsylvania, and has joined us for several Pittsburgh Pirates games at PNC.

I was excited to join the family for these games because I know how passionate they are about baseball, and I wanted to spend time as a family unit. It was always nice to take up a big section of the stadium and bond with the family over baseball.

My favorite memory from our trips to the stadium was getting to talk to the family and enjoy some down time. It was always relaxing to sit and watch the game. Also, the food! One of my favorite memories was when we all went to the Pirates game and had box seats. It was ninety degrees outside, so we all stayed inside. My dad and I always get wings, and we asked Pap Pap if he wanted to try some...we thought he would decline, and he ate almost the whole box!

I learned a lot about individual players. I am not good with names, so these experiences have taught me who some of the big players were and are. Also, I learned about what players my family members liked the most. Raise the Jolly Roger!

Deanna C. and Joel S., Dayna's sister (who is a CPA) and brother-in-law (he's a news anchor), live in Myrtle Beach, South Carolina and have joined us for several games.

Sometimes we've just attended games because the family was going to be together anyway for the weekend, and we thought it would be fun. When we joined the family for the Homerun Derby, we were going to be passing through Minneapolis on our way to visit Joel's mother in Iowa, and we had never been to a Homerun Derby or Fanfest. We thought it would be fun to join the Haferkamps for the day.

Some of our favorite memories from these trips were at the Pirates game. We were impressed that we could stay inside the stadium lounge area and relax and watch the game. DeeDee was excited about being able to see Manny Sanguillén, one of her favorite players when she was growing up. He autographed her baseball jersey. The most memorable part of the Home Run Derby was the cold weather. It was freezing, even though it was July! The good part about that was that DeeDee bought an All Star blanket to stay warm, and she cherishes it to this day. It was fun to watch the boys participate in the Fanfest activities, and Joel had a good time being a pretend baseball announcer.

We enjoy the game food, like hot dogs, bratwursts, pretzels, and so on. DeeDee loved her hot dog at the Homerun Derby with the words "All Star" spelled out in ketchup! Also, it's always fun to see the kids enjoying themselves at the game and rooting for their baseball heroes. Since we didn't know many of the players at the Homerun Derby, it was great to have Grant and Jack filling us in on the players and all their stats.

Alan A., Steve's college friend, is a realtor who lives in Atlanta, Georgia, brought his daughter and met us for an Atlanta Braves game.

When I got the call from the Haferkamps, and they said they were on a national stadium tour and planned to visit Atlanta, I knew I was the man for the job! They wanted to visit an Atlanta Braves game at Turner Field, and I was ecstatic. First, it had been a while since I had seen my good friends. The last time I recalled seeing them was in San Diego at their home, during one of my business or pleasure trips. Several years had passed, and our families had both gained some small additional members. And oh, how I enjoy getting that awesome annual holiday card summarizing the Haferkamps' year, always with that baseball theme. Watching their kids grow and seeing those holiday cards made me realize how much they enjoy baseball and how it had become such a big topic in their lives. Likewise, my daughter has come up through the ranks in softball at our local Sandy Springs, Georgia community and her school leagues, where she pitches and plays various positions pretty much year-round.

Being native to Atlanta, where I too played in my first Little League, I have so many memories of the Atlanta Braves, 1996 Olympics, and all the various events around the stadiums and downtown Atlanta, and I was excited to share them with my friends!

As a child, on special occasions we would all go to the Braves games as a family. I remember the Braves National Championship in the 90s, and still remember that TV host saying, "Braves win, Braves win, Braves win!" and running around chanting, tomahawking in a train with twenty of my college friends. What a great memory that is!

I learned how proud I am of my home team. I will now soon witness the demolition of Turner Field, and I'll get to experience yet another new stadium, soon to be built in Cobb County. Not many can say they attended opening events in three major stadiums in their hometown in their lifetime...and I am still young.

As you can see, it's surprising how effective of a reunion tool a baseball game is. Old friends that you haven't seen in a long time can be difficult to invite out, for example, for drinks at a bar or to dinner. A baseball game is easy; it gives you and your company a common element to bond over, and it can be enjoyed by those from all walks of life, at any stage.

Friends that we hadn't talked to since college, former clients—we would just send out messages to say, hey, we're going to be in your town! It was just terrific, we saw a lot of people who normally we wouldn't be able to see. We included a lot of people.

It was great; during our planning stages, we would just sit down and think about people we would love to see, who we still kept in touch with through holiday cards and online. It provided a wonderful opportunity for learning new things and making new connections. We didn't have a million friends join us, and we didn't offer it to everybody over the Internet or whatever, just people that we kept in touch with. This trip was special to us, and we wanted to share it with people who would also join in for our special memories. This is a good way to reconnect. It's a great thing to experience with family and friends that you see a lot, but also great for reinvigorating old friendships.

We would simply call up friends and ask them if they wanted to catch their home team play ball on a certain day. Those we asked were generally pleasantly surprised and agreed, when they might not have if the plan was something more usual. All in all, it turned out to be an excellent way to reconnect. From cousins to fraternity brothers, baseball offers something anyone can enjoy. You can really get people there to go with you, you just have to ask!

Although we treasure our memories and mementos from our games with all our friends, we were careful to keep our official picture book to just family. We thought about certain things as special keepsakes that can be passed down, and we wanted permanent reminders of spending the time with the people we are closest to.

The type of bond created between us and our family members and friends who were able to share in our journey, takes some effort, logistically, to accomplish. From the onset, we knew that we wanted to have people along with us on this adventure. We are so grateful we did it; we created memories that we will all carry with us forever. Some of the older members of our family often times thought they wouldn't be able to make the trips, but then when it came down to it, they would go, and they were so glad that they did, for those great memories. Dayna's father, who is in his eighties, still mentions how much he enjoyed meeting us in D.C. for a game. Washington D.C. has always been a special place for Dayna's parents, because they had lived there and worked for Capital Airlines when they were newly married in 1948.

We made a point of sending out an invitation via email well before the game, so that as many who wanted to join would be able to, and learned early to make attending a game with us as stress-free and enjoyable as possible for the people we invited. By creating an event around it, like hiring a bus to take a group of people, it just makes it all that much more special than everyone going on their own in their cars. It creates a whole experience outside of the game. You can get extended S.U.V.s from limousine companies; there are lots of opportunities to rent vehicles that will take a whole bunch of your friends and family to the game. If you were looking to spend a little bit of extra money to celebrate a birthday or something, it's definitely something to look into. It makes the experience a lot more appealing, if you've got twenty people going down and you don't have to park eight cars, because usually everybody would have to worry about where to park and how much parking will cost. It takes some of the stress out of the situation, and creates your own unique tailgating experience! It just makes it a little bit easier for people to say, "Sure, that sounds great!" It also guarantees that the event doesn't end on a sour note—we've driven out of many sports stadiums after a game, and it can take forever and be very frustrating.

Group baseball games are also a great way to make an already special occasion even more exciting. Visiting a stadium to see a ballgame as a family is also an excellent way to celebrate a birthday that falls during the season, for example. Both Jack and Pap Pap have birthdays in late July, and celebrating them at the ballpark when we were able to was always a special treat! There is no clean up, the entertainment is provided, and there is time and space to enjoy everyone who might come.

Take the opportunity to make connections with family members and friends that you otherwise would not have, and create special memories that will last forever. It's well worth the planning!

Although every baseball team travels far and wide, playing eighty-one away games each season, some teams have moved far from their original homes over the course of their club history. Out of the five MLB teams in California (the Angels, Dodgers, Athletics, Padres, and Giants), three of them are transplants, originally from the East Coast, like us. When we're missing our extended families and friends back home, it helps our family to go root on a nearby team who can understand carving out new traditions in sunny California. Finishing up a whirlwind tour of stadiums far from home and meeting up with family and friends scattered across the U.S., we personally ended the 2013 baseball season with a great short trip less than three hours north of our home to Los Angeles, to see the Dodgers take on the Reds.

Like so many other teams, the Los Angeles Dodgers haven't always been in their current home town. Originally, they hail from New York City. The early history of the Dodgers has a lot in common with that of the Pirates. Like the Pirates, the Dodgers were originally known by a different name: the Brooklyn Atlantics, and later the Trolley Dodgers. Also like the Pirates, they switched from the American Association to the National League. They did this in 1890, several years after the Pirates had made the switch.

The team name was eventually shortened to just "the Dodgers," and they played at Dodger Memorial Stadium for many years. The Dodgers were actually the first team to fight against segregation in professional baseball when they signed Jackie Robinson in 1947. Robinson would become an iconic figure in baseball history not only because he was the first African-American to play pro ball, but because he was a phenomenal player. He won Rookie of the Year that year, and would go on to help the Dodgers defeat the Yankees in the 1955 World Series. A many-time All-Star, MVP, and NL batting champion, Robinson was inducted into the Hall of Fame in 1962. He was also the first player in any professional sport to have his number, 42, retired across all teams in 1997. Since then, his memory has been further honored on Jackie Robinson Day (April 15th), where *all* players wear the number 42!

Due to the efforts of great players like Robinson, the Dodgers had a very successful tenure in New York. They were one of the strongest teams in the National League for most of the 1940s and 1950s, and around 1955 team management started looking at locations for a new stadium. The stadium the Dodgers had been playing at, Ebbets Field, was very old and needed replacing. The Dodgers were denied use of land by city officials, and the team began considering a move.

The move ended up being much farther than they had originally had in mind, as the first buyers who approached the team were based in Los Angeles. The country was changing, and the business world had in mind a future where professional sporting events would be held all over the country, and fans would travel by air. In 1958, the first commercial airliner, the Boeing 707, would enter use, and make this world possible. After getting word of this possible move, the New York Giants expressed an interest in a similar move. So, in 1957 the announcement was made that the Brooklyn Dodgers and New York Giants would be moving to California. This shift from east to west was a pivotal event in MLB history.

After three seasons at the Los Angeles Memorial Coliseum, the Dodgers moved into Dodger Stadium, where they play to this day. When we visited the stadium for the first time in 2013, the age of the venue was readily apparent, in a good way. Stadium management decided some time ago to embrace the old-time feel of the park. For example, in 2005, the stadium underwent extensive renovations and all the seats were replaced with seats that matched the original 1962 color. We were struck right away by the cool, retro vibe of the place.

This isn't to say that Dodger Stadium is trapped in the past! Modern baseball fans love their Jumbotrons, and being able to see them during the game is a huge factor for some. Dodger Stadium and the Oakland Coliseum are unique in that they have two identically sized Jumbotrons over left and right field, so that the maximum number of fans can enjoy them. The Dodgers' Jumbotrons are also very new, and have incredibly sharp displays.

The view from upper level seating is breathtaking, particularly of the Santa Monica Mountains. Everything feels airy and wide open, and the weather is almost always perfect. The food is great, and we just had to try the famous "Dodger dogs." They are hotdogs, nearly a foot long, that have been enjoyed by Dodgers fans for decades.

The game didn't go so well for the Dodgers, but the baseball was still fantastic. We were also established Reds' fans then, and the Dodgers had just had a great winning streak, so the day was a success. We saw a few home runs, and got to witness another excellent performance from a Reds' pitcher, this time Mat Latos. It was also Vin Scully bobblehead night, so we got to add another to our collection! Scully is one of the best-loved broadcasters in MLB, and has been calling games for the Dodgers for over sixty years.

Chris Withrow, the Dodger pitcher, and Jay Bruce, right fielder for the Reds, both threw the boys balls. The boys also got a few autographs from the outfield, and had a special chance meeting with Jerry Hairston Jr. You can never know when being in the right place at the right time will lead to a great baseball relationship. A few months earlier, we had bumped into Hairston of the Dodgers at Petco, in the Park in the Park during an off-day.

It was during spring break, and Steve had brought some kids down to the Park at the Park to kill time and toss balls around. The Dodgers were coming into town, and there was a baseball mood in the air. While the boys were playing whiffle ball, he went over to a nearby taco place, Lolita's, to buy them lunch. On his way back, he noticed an adult had joined them and was playing. At first Steve was a little wary, but when he got closer, the boys all rushed him, babbling about a major league player who was hanging out with them.

Sure enough, it was Hairston! He had played for the Padres a while ago, and was now with the Dodgers and in town for the series. He had been walking over to Lolita's as well, saw a bunch of kids playing ball, and couldn't resist. Steve and Grant told him about our plan to tour all the stadiums, and so on, and he said that when we were at Dodger Stadium we should come down and holler at him to say hello. Jerry's brother Scott also played for the Padres, and we are always fans of brothers on the field!

Jerry is a really fascinating person, and an interesting player—he played every position in the game except pitcher and catcher before he retired in 2013! He was great to the boys, and we really enjoyed talking to him. At the Dodgers-Reds game, we went down near the dugout before the game, and he came over to chat with us again and say hello to the boys. This time, they had balls ready, and scored some autographs. It was a wonderful way to end the season and a great short trip, connecting with new friends on the field, and always remembering how our baseball journey helps strengthen our family.

We can't close out this chapter about family without a nod to one of the other California teams that we love, the Oakland Athletics. The A's have become very important to our family, as you will find out in a later chapter!

One of the regular season games that we went to at Oakland Coliseum featured the A's playing against the Astros. Oakland Coliseum is one of the older stadiums in use, construction having finished in 1966. During the spring and summer, it hosts baseball games, and during the fall and winter, fans can catch the home games of the Oakland Raiders football team. Oakland Coliseum is actually the last stadium in the country that still hosts both professional football and baseball games. Some, like Wrigley field (which once hosted both Bears football and Cubs baseball) were converted to single-use stadiums.

Some may say that the Oakland Coliseum is on the older side, and that modifications made over the years have made it a less and less attractive place to catch a baseball game, but we loved our time spent at this game, and are incredibly thankful to the service people there. It was world class! The day of the Athletics' game against the Astros, they went out of their way to direct us to prime locations for autographs. We had brought a wooden bat that day, and ended up getting a number of autographs... probably the most we have gotten in a single day! We will talk more about techniques for getting autographs in a later chapter.

We got a number of great autographs from the home team. We got to meet Yoenis Céspedes, winner of the Home Run Derby we attended in 2014, switch-hitting Coco Crisp, and pitcher Jesse Chavez. This was a great start to a special relationship we have and cherish with the A's and Oakland Coliseum.

We got some autographs from the visiting team as well. The Houston Astros had been in last place the year before this game, and no one had been paying much attention to them. They turned around and stocked up on quality players from their minor league team, and now these younger players made up a great team. They had a breakout year, and we got the bat signed by a lot of these talented young players!

Jerome Williams was one. He is a funny guy, and has been traded to a bunch of different teams. He is incredibly friendly, and talked to everybody who came up to him. He is easy to recognize on the mound because he has a pink glove and a pink necklace, which he wears in honor of his mom, who has breast cancer. At a different game he flicked us a couple balls when we were there early.

Another big script was from Chris Carter, a very talented first baseman. George Springer was another, and he had just been called up for his MLB debut shortly before. The boys actually got his attention by yelling, "Welcome to the show!" in congratulations when they saw him. He got off to a great start with a very solid first year. Finally, the boys were really happy that José Altuve, something of an expert at stealing bases, was gracious enough to sign.

Many thanks to all these guys and more, for proving the naysayers wrong, showing that the magic of baseball is alive and well in Oakland. Both the Raiders and A's are looking at new sites for stadiums, and even new cities, but we are very glad we got to spend some time in one of the oldest West Coast ballparks, and hope they stay.

The game itself was a thrilling one if you were an A's fan, and on that day, we were! It featured a dominant performance from the home team, as the Athletics hit several home runs in the first inning alone, climbing to an early 7-0 lead. It was one of the highest scoring first innings we have ever seen! The Astros didn't get blown out completely, though, and the final score was 11 to 3.

Sometimes games are slow, strategic ones that unfold over the course of several hours, and sometimes they are offensive firecrackers, with home runs and errors galore. We like them both! We hope that this chapter has given you an idea of how important baseball is to our family, and how it serves as a unique way to strengthen bonds with those you love. We also hope that it inspires you to call up friends and family of your own, and to see what wonderful experiences are right around the corner for you!

CHAPTER THREE
No-Hitter

Attending a game with friends and family is always time well spent, and sometimes you get the chance to experience something truly special within the sport itself. We have been taken pleasantly by surprise several times. We have always been thankful, after certain games, to have been with loved ones and seen the best baseball has to offer. One of these moments occurred during our trip to see the Reds play in their hometown of Cincinnati, Ohio.

The Reds' stadium, Great American Ballpark, became Grant's favorite ballpark during our trip, and for good reason—even though things didn't start off so swimmingly! The first day we were in Cincinnati, the boys attended a game with their Uncle Dean and ended up being rained out. They were certainly not going down easily, and Dean remembers being the last group of people to take cover and amongst the last fans in the stands. The weather had been fierce, with driving winds and heavy rain that forced the attendees to don red ponchos. The downpour eventually got bad enough that the game was called in the sixth inning, with the Reds winning against the San Francisco Giants. Dean, Steve, and the boys actually had to trudge some distance back to the hotel, since the shuttle they hopped on couldn't get close because of high water! They eventually stumbled back to the hotel soaking wet, and flash flood warnings set off alerts on everyone's phones throughout the night.

The same teams were supposed to be playing the next night, as part of a series: the San Francisco Giants and the at-home Cincinnati

Reds. When we stepped off the hotel bus at the Marriott that night, there was at least eight inches of water to slog through. We didn't even know if they were going to be able to have the game the next day, as stadium management wasn't sure that they could have the field properly drained in time. They did, thankfully, because the game we saw that day, on July 2, 2013, was one of the best we have ever been to!

We began the day with a tour of the stadium. The weather was now perfect, but the tour guides pointed out several areas where the previous evening's torrential downpour had caused damage to the stadium, gushing through walkways and down staircases. It didn't diminish our appreciation for the beauty of the field! We actually had a very special, and funny, moment during this tour. We were on one of the lower levels of the stadium. The tour guide had a great sense of humor and was definitely enjoying himself. He really had the tourists' attention and we were all getting a lot out of the tour, when we all heard the unmistakable *click clack* of baseball cleats on a hard floor. As we turned around, the tour guide said, "Well, here are the San Francisco Giants," as though they were just another part of the tour. And sure enough, there they were: fifteen Giants players in uniform on their way to the locker room. Of course, everyone on the tour just kind of stared, wide-eyed, while the poor tour guide kept trying to get us back on track by saying, "Okay, okay, everyone...there is nothing to see here, folks!" He was very dedicated, but when the starting lineup of the San Francisco Giants walk by, no baseball fan is going to pay attention to anything else. Obviously the guide didn't want everyone to bombard the players, and between his efforts and the sheer shock at so many great players being within arms' reach, they made it to the locker room without anyone thinking to rush over and ask for autographs, but not before Grant got away with a wave from All-Star third-baseman Pablo Sandoval. The tour, the no-hitter, the food...the Reds' stadium was a fantastic experience from start to finish.

Opened in 2003, the Great American Ballpark is an example of what can be accomplished, architecturally and artistically, in a modern stadium. There are works of art scattered throughout the stadium, including several large mosaics depicting important events in Reds' history that will be of interest to fans of both baseball and art. *The Great Eight* mosaic depicts the starting roster of the legendary 1975 Cincinnati Reds, featuring renowned players like Ken Griffey, Sr. This team was one of the most successful and winningest in MLB history, posting a sterling 108-54 record and winning Cincinnati's first World Series title since 1940. The other mosaic displays some of the members of the 1869 "Red Stockings." The modern day Reds team has the distinction of being the descendants of the first professional baseball team in North America. An outgrowth of the Cincinnati Base Ball Club formed in 1866, the Red Stockings were the first fully salaried baseball team in the United States, as well as the only team to ever post a perfect season: 65-0 in their first year. When you are the only team paying all the members, it appears you attract only the best!

Along with these mosaics, art, baseball, and history buffs can find a number of interesting statues throughout the park. They are very popular locations for photos, especially the ones in front of the main entrance to the stadium. The crowning piece to this famous gallery of baseball art is *The Spirit of Baseball*, a massive mural carved out of solid limestone that graces the western corner of the Reds' administrative building. This mural speaks to all generations of baseball players. It features a child with a bat dreaming of professional play, represented by three players in the clouds above the Cincinnati waterfront. If you can manage it, check out the mural at night after it is lit from below by several floodlights. It is an awe-inspiring sculpture, and even more striking when the sun has set.

The stadium is interesting architecturally as well. It is a relatively small ballpark, but the dimensions are well used and the general effect seems cozy and warm, while still being open. In the stands, between third base and home, you will find the famous "Gap," a break in the seating that affords fans an incredible view of the Cincinnati skyline and signature smokestacks from within the stadium. From out in the city, if you were to look right down Sycamore Street, you would be able to see directly into the stadium. It runs along the Ohio River, and the riverboats are beautiful. It is easy to understand why, while on the tour, we saw a young man propose to his shocked bride-to-be right on the field! It is a picturesque park, that's for sure.

After the tour, we ate at the Holy Grail, an excellent restaurant across from the stadium that is famous for its Reuben Egg Rolls and wide selection of beer. After a few fantastic burgers, we went to meet up with some extended family: Steve's cousin Doug and his family. We had actually never met his whole family, so it was wonderful being able to get to know them on the road and share what would end up being the most memorable day of our journey!

The game started off like any other as we settled into our seats. Well, not quite like any other—Dayna was pleasantly surprised to have her wine served in an actual wineglass, rather than the usual plastic cup.

The Reds pitcher, Homer Bailey, had had a middling season so far, and was sporting a record slightly below .500. He had, however, ended the previous season on a high note, having pitched the last no-hitter of the regular season against the Pirates. A no-hitter is a game during which a pitcher doesn't allow an opposing player to first base by means of a hit. One or two no-hitters occur during each regular season, and they are always an exciting achievement that no baseball fan would want to miss.

In the first inning, Bailey struck out the first of the San Francisco batters, and the next two were out after hitting a pair of harmless fly balls that were easily nabbed by the Reds' outfield. Something similar happened in the second and third innings, by which point we could pick out some of the most dedicated baseball fans paying extra attention to the game. Partway through the fourth inning, the Giants were still without a single hit. Grant leaned over to Dayna and whispered, "Mom, this guy is pitching a perfect game!"

A perfect game is one of the rarest, most exciting events in professional baseball. In over one hundred years of play, there have only been twenty-three of them. To achieve a perfect game, a team must prevent the other team from getting a player safely to first base. Any walks or hits ruin a perfect game. There can be no players hit by pitches, and no home runs. Perfect games, and those close to them, are ultimately a team effort, but they are considered one of the premier achievements for pitchers in particular. To face twenty-seven batters, and keep all of them from getting a good enough hit to get through the infield and outfield, is something every pitcher dreams of.

This game was no exception to the defense rule. While Bailey was striking out batters, his teammates were backing him up by making defensive plays when needed. By the end of the sixth inning, the entire stadium was buzzing. Eighteen Giants batters had gone up to the plate, and eighteen Giants batters had returned to the dugout with nothing to show for their time. Doug would later name this as his favorite memory of attending games with us, and describe how the building excitement, inning after inning, was something wonderful to experience with family.

The dream of a perfect game ended in the seventh inning, however, when Homer walked Gregor Blanco, one of the Giants' outfielders. The possibility of a perfect game was downgraded to that of a no-hitter. To make matters more intense for the players, and more exciting for the crowd, this walk occurred on a full count, when Bailey was just a single pitch away from striking out yet another batter and continuing on the path to pitching perfection. The atmosphere was still electric, and we wouldn't have been surprised to find out that even a few Giants' fans were secretly rooting for an historic outcome.

During the seventh inning we also saw, on top of the thrilling events of the game thus far, a brilliant defensive play from Joey Votto, the Reds' first baseman. Buster Posey, his counterpart on the Giants' roster, hit a tricky ball between first and second, breaking his bat in the process. Votto jumped on the ball right away, but Bailey had misjudged the distance the ball would travel and was too far away to make it to first to get the last out of the inning. Votto, with his eyes on the whole field, saw a chance to save the no-hitter, and instead of trying to get the out at first, launched the ball to Frasier on third. Blanco had already committed from second and was gunning for third, and Frasier was able to tag him out. It was a sensational play, and the Reds fans in the crowd roared in appreciation.

The crowd was completely behind Bailey at this point, even if he had given up a walk. Each passing play saw a slight uptick in the volume of our cheers, and the energy with which we all shot up out of our seats to high-five one another. Our group joined the rest of the stadium at the close of the eighth inning, standing up to applaud the performance. We were, to say the least, thrilled! While we have our favorite teams, we usually end up adopting and rooting for the home team on our travels to their stadiums. The fact that Bailey was pitching such an amazing game at home made it that much sweeter for us!

The first out of the ninth inning was due to quick thinking on the part of Bailey himself, when he jumped to catch a skipping line drive. The crowd loved it! The second out of the ninth was another strikeout, Bailey's ninth and last of the game. The final out was off a simple drive to third base, and an easy toss to first. For the second time in the span of a few months, Homer Bailey had made history. After that final out, the Reds dugout rushed the mound, clamoring and surrounding Bailey in celebration. It is often said that "the crowd went wild," but in this case, it actually had! Amidst fireworks, Bailey's teammates continued to swarm him, dousing him in Gatorade and hugging him, huge grins on every face. It was a wonderful thing to experience, both as a family and as individual fans of baseball.

As the excitement began to settle and we made our way out of the stadium, Jack mentioned that there had only been 275 no-hitters in MLB history. We were impressed that he knew this fact, and we remain continually amazed by the knowledge of the game both of our boys have picked up over the course of our journey. They were also quick to point out that since Bailey had only allowed a single walk, on a full count, he had technically been only one pitch away from throwing the twenty-fourth perfect game in professional baseball history!

Another interesting fact about this no-hitter was that it had been the first of the season. This meant that Bailey had thrown the last no-hitter of the previous season, and the first no-hitter of the current season. It's a rare feat in baseball, and it hadn't happened since the legendary Nolan Ryan accomplished it in 1975. That day, Bailey had also earned the distinction of becoming only the third Red to throw more than one career no-hitter, following in the footsteps of Jim Maloney and Johnny Vander Meer. There was so much to enjoy about this game, and we spent a portion of the next day gathering up local newspapers, all of which featured Bailey in some frozen moment of triumph on the front page. We have them still, and they will remain one of our most treasured collections.

There was, however, one small blemish on an otherwise perfect day. The boys had started collecting baseball cards very early on, and Grant had brought about fifteen or so Reds cards with him, hoping to get some signed. Amidst the excitement of the no-hitter, he placed them in the cup holder to his seat and quickly forgot about them. He left them there when we exited the stadium, as we were all talking about and celebrating the game and had other things on our minds! By the time he realized they were missing, we were long gone. He was very disappointed to have left them, and despite checking with lost and found several times, we were never able to get the cards back. At the end of the day though, it was a trade that he would make again! If forced to pick a favorite team, Grant would probably go with the Cincinnati Reds, because of how amazing this game was, and how great the Reds have been to us at spring training, which we will talk about in a later chapter.

We were lucky enough to experience many other exciting baseball moments over the course of our adventure, including grand slams and walk-off home runs, thrilling victories and stunning defeats. One of the very first games we took the boys to together, when Jack was about a year old, was particularly memorable. We mentioned it in the first chapter, and here is what happened. It was in 2006, and was another game between our two "family" teams: the home Padres and the visiting Pirates.

In professional baseball, there is a concept in pitching called "closing" or "saving." A "closer" is a pitcher who is particularly skilled at getting the final outs needed to finish off a game when his team is winning. A "save" occurs when a closer meets certain requirements and finishes out the game by recording a victory for his team. There are a number of requirements, among them the fact that the closer must also not have been pitcher when his team took the lead, and must pitch at least one inning. At the time of this game, the Padres closer, Trevor Hoffman, was one game away from scoring his 479th save, which would be the record for all-time career saves. The previous record, held by Lee Smith, had been in place since 1993.

Over the course of the previous seasons, a tradition had developed at Petco Park known as "Trevor Time." Whenever the record-hunting Hoffman came onto the field to close the game, the crowd would go crazy and "Hells Bells" by ACDC would blast over the stadium-wide sound system. An image of a flickering fire would appear on the Jumbotron, and as Hoffman stepped up to the mound, the other team could sense that they were doomed. For months, there had been a series of placards off the higher level seating of the Metal Supply Co. Building, counting down the saves until the record was broken. The home crowd loved Trevor Time, and a sold-out crowd took to its feet as he went onto the field that sunny day in September.

We had been fans of both the Padres and Trevor for a number of years, and Grant had been to several games before, but this was the first time his little brother had been able to come with us, and our good friend Lea joined us too. It was a great, electric experience. We were sitting very high up, and had a great view of everything: the field, the crowd, the Jumbotron, the countdown signs. Even the skyline was oddly picturesque, as it was a clear day and you could see the growing buildings of the city scattered about the stadium. The score was 2 to 1, and Trevor came on to pitch out the ninth inning. He retired the first batter in four pitches, finishing off with a speedy ball right down the middle that the Pirate didn't even swing for. The second batter was sent packing after a swing and a miss at a blazing fastball on a full count. The third batter hit a line drive to third that was scooped up and sent to first with time to spare. Trevor Hoffman had broken the record! The countdown placards were removed to reveal signs that proudly proclaimed his achievement, ACDC was back in the air, and Jack experienced his first historic baseball moment. Hoffman had done it, and he had done it in style, needing a mere fourteen pitches to retire the only three Pirates batters he faced. Trevor would retire in 2010, still the record holder, and we would go on with the newest young baseball fan to many more games!

There are certain events in baseball that have an almost magical quality to them. Grand slams, triple plays, a player outwitting the infield to steal home—these are all things that even the youngest kids find fascinating about the game. We were lucky enough, over the course of seeing a lot of games, to witness our fair share of these moments. We've said it before, but it bears repeating; baseball is a wonderfully rich game, and there is no telling when you will see something historic or unusual.

Some of the last stadiums we went to were dotted around the Midwest, where baseball traditions run quite deep. We had managed to fit a game into our schedule that allowed us to see our Pirates again, this time as the away team against the Cardinals in Saint Louis.

The Saint Louis Cardinals are one of the oldest clubs in North America, and can trace their roots to the latter half of the nineteenth century. Of course, like most of the other old clubs, they saw several name changes before they became the team we know today. They were originally known, before incorporation as a major league team, by several names inspired by their brown stockings. In 1900, they changed their name from the Browns to the Cardinals. They are not to be confused with the Saint Louis Browns, who played in the same city from 1902 to 1953, and had once been the Milwaukee Brewers and would eventually become the Baltimore Orioles!

Along with these complicated naming and geographical issues, there is the history of the Cardinals' home stadium. The Cardinals have played in many parks over the years, and several of them have shared the name of the park that we visited in 2014: Busch Stadium. The modern Busch is a gorgeous structure, primarily constructed out of striking red brick. It is as large as it is beautiful, and can fit just shy of 50,000 for the biggest of games. Its location on Clark Avenue allows for one of the most impressive ballpark views in the country, and St. Louis is a town that takes its baseball seriously—it is one of the easiest to access on public transit. From the very edge of the nosebleed seats behind and above home plate, Busch offers a stunning view of downtown St. Louis, including an almost complete view of the famous Arch.

We actually have a unique connection to the stadium, one that made the trip more personal for us. Steve's parents had been close friends with John J. Smith, founder and owner of the masonry company that had built the stadium and ballpark village, for many years. He had been a wonderful friend of the family and the biggest Cardinals fan we knew, and would pass away a few months after we had had such a fantastic time at his beautiful stadium. We will always remember him and the work he did to ensure that generations of fans would be able to enjoy the game at Busch.

Once inside the stadium, there is plenty to do and see both before and after the game. There are a number of statues throughout the park, many of which originally graced the previous Busch Stadium (known as Busch Memorial Stadium), which had served the team from 1966 to 2005 on the same physical site. Some of the statues are interesting in part because they are so lifelike; they depict several famous players from Cardinals history in the middle of the action. Rogers Hornsby, one of the most accurate batters in major league history, is forever sending a ball over the fence, his bat pointing outwards towards the stands. Hall of Fame inductee Lou Brock is just tossing aside his bat; he is at the beginning of the sprint to first base. These statues form an arc around the entrance to the stadium housing the main Cardinals store, and make a profound impression on first viewing.

It was a night game, but as it was mid-July, the air was clear and pleasantly warm. The game had been a very tightly contested affair thus far, with the Cardinals taking an early lead after some solid hitting by rookie Kolten Wong in the second inning. After the Pirates had caught up in the fourth, both teams scored a pair of runs in the fifth. Going into the ninth inning, the game was still tied 4 to 4. The stage was set; Wong was back at the plate, staring down a full count, with two outs registered. The Pirates had failed to score during the top of the ninth, so everything came down to this last pitch. The Pirates pitcher let the ball fly, and it zipped right through the middle of the strike zone, where Wong hit it directly. Everyone within earshot could tell the ball was going over the fence based just on the sound; it was that pure, crisp *crack* that only comes from a perfect connection, sweet spot to sweet spot. The crowd started to roar as the ball rose higher and higher, easily clearing the fence.

The home team had won with a walk-off home run—two nights in a row! This game had been part of a series, and the previous night the Cardinals had tallied a 2 to 0 win after Adams hit a walk-off homer of his own. Walk-off home runs aren't an incredibly rare occurrence, but they aren't necessarily common either, and for the home team to manage two in a row...that was amazing. We weren't able to see the first game, since we were in the middle of one of our most tightly scheduled summer tours, but we were glad to make the more exciting night! The crew was ready, and fireworks rose into the sky as Wong rounded second base. His teammates had already run to home plate to congratulate him. It was also the first walk-off homer of Wong's career, hit at the most dramatic time in a ball game. The cheers from the at-capacity home crowd were long and loud. We were happy to have seen the game with our dear friends in Saint Louis. We were, of course, sad to see that our Pirates had lost, but Steve put it best when he said, "There's nothing Wong with that!" as the ball found its target over four hundred feet from home plate.

And there wasn't. Part of being a baseball fan is acknowledging that every team's stirring victory is a heartbreaking defeat for the opponent. For every thrilling home run, there is a disappointed pitcher. Every lucky bounce for the visiting team is an unlucky one for the home team. As fans, we have a unique perspective, and see the whole game for what it is, in a way the players, as highly invested professionals, might not: a small piece of a larger, wonderful history that we are lucky to be witness to. No matter the outcome of the game, our hats are off to the players, manager, and stadium crew that make the magic happen!

Every ballpark in the major leagues is different as far as playing conditions are concerned, and this has a huge impact on the play you will see. This dynamic contributes to the richness of the sport in general, particularly for those who might want to visit each stadium and see all of the entertaining possibilities. Professional stadiums in other sports are often very similar. They have the same dimensions within the playing area and it equalizes the achievements made, regardless of the space— for example, in football, a thirty-yard touchdown pass at FedExField is much the same as a thirty yard pass at Heinz Field. Professional baseball has a much longer and deeper tradition in North America than professional football or basketball, and consequently boasts some of the oldest stadiums still in use. Regulations over the past hundred years weren't always what they are now, and as a result, no two ballparks are the same. Keeping with this tradition, baseball isn't nearly as stringent in their actual regulations for the fields, and there is considerably more leeway for individual teams and cities to build even new ballparks with various specifications that fit the history of the individual teams and their historic energy and preferred mode of play.

For example, the Angel Stadium of Anaheim was built in 1966, and the distance from home plate to the center field fence is 396 feet. Fenway Park, finished in 1912, boasts an extra twenty-four feet for the same dimension. To hit a home run straight down center field is extremely difficult, no matter the circumstances, but it takes a little bit more power to do it at Fenway. The left field fence at Nationals Park is 336 feet away. Back at Fenway, that distance is a mere 310 feet, but the fence is nearly thirty feet higher and a lovely shade of green. This aptly-named "Green Monster" makes a left-field homer a special event at Fenway, something that will add a little extra excitement and uniqueness to a trip there.

These sorts of quirks make tours of the ballparks interesting in a way that is unique to baseball. Each stadium has its own character, implicit in the architecture and bolstered by decades of fandom, to really give each experience a life of its own. In many cases, the size and shape of the stadium puts a unique spin on the playstyle and results one is likely to see. For example, the Oakland Coliseum, home to the Oakland As, features foul territory significantly larger than any other park. This makes it a very pitcher-friendly park, since the infielders are able to snag more foul balls than usual for some easy outs. There are other stadiums that even have specialized rules, made necessary by quirks in the playing field. Tropicana Field, home to the Tampa Bay Rays, is a covered stadium that uses a less-than-ideal form of cable suspension to support the dome. There are four large rings of catwalks that help keep the dome in place, which are frequently hit by pop up flies. The twist is that the ball is ruled in or out of play based on which of the ringed catwalks it hits, and what area of the ring is hit! As one can imagine, several times a ball hitting a catwalk has affected the outcome of a game, leading to numerous complaints from teams and fans. Temporary changes to those rules have taken place over the years. If you are lucky, you might even see a player hit a home run that blows out a lightbulb way up there!

Wrigley Field is another ballpark subject to unique rulings. Wrigley is one of the oldest fields still in use at the professional level, having been completed in 1914, and is held in special regard by many fans. One of its most iconic features is the brick wall that serves as the entirety of the outfield fence. The wall was part of the original construction, and ivy was planted along its base in 1937. That ivy grows to this day, and over the course of each baseball season transforms from a series of thin, green vines to a flourishing barricade of leaves. At full growth, the ivy wall can very easily make a ball vanish after a hit deep into the outfield, which will often result in a ground rule double. A ground rule double is a special ruling from the umpire that occurs after a ball has gone from in-play status after a pitch to out-of-play status. It is called a "double" because it allows for each player on base, including the batter at home, to move two full bases forward.

As crazy as things can be now at certain stadiums, they were even crazier in years past. Target Field, home of the Minnesota Twins, was one of the very last stadiums we visited. If we had slated the team in earlier in our game-going career, we might have caught a game at the Hubert H. Humphrey Metrodome, which hosted its last (baseball) season in 2009 and was torn down in 2014.

The "H.H.H." Metrodome was an odd stadium. It acted for some time as home to the Minnesota football team, the Vikings, and also hosted basketball and soccer events. No stadium can effectively host all of these different sports, and there were some minor disasters relating to the design of the space that affected baseball games played there. Matt Lawton, outfielder for the Twins for several years, was famously hit right in the face by an easy fly ball after he was blinded by the notoriously bright lights and lost sight of the ball against the equally-white background of the dome. Fielding wasn't the only thing that could be a nightmare! Speakers suspended from the dome robbed players of home runs on several occasions when the ball bounced off them, and at least one hit ball never even came down after sailing up into the glowing heights. Target Field is certainly impressive, and one of the most futuristic stadiums we visited, but we do wish we could have spent time at this other unique and wonderful stadium.

The material that is used in the fields themselves has also varied greatly over the years. AstroTurf took the professional sporting world by storm in the 70s and 80s, only to eventually be phased out of the major leagues by natural grass again, or FieldTurf, a much improved alternative to AstroTurf. AstroTurf taught players during its heyday to expect the ball to bounce higher and skip faster, a lesson slightly unlearned since the reconversion. It is entirely possible that the two remaining fields using artificial turf, Rogers Centre and Tropicana Field, will see some trickier than usual defensive plays because of their turf composition.

As you travel from ballpark to ballpark, you will even run into stadiums that have unique features that are outside human control. Coors Field opened its doors in 1995 as the "tallest" stadium in major league baseball, rising up into the thin Colorado air at 5,280 feet (mile high) above sea level. Purple seats ring around the stadium, marking the "mile high" level. Players quickly found that in thin, dry air at high elevation, a hit baseball will travel much farther than normal. This led to a period of time when miserable pitchers were ruled over by happy batters in the Rocky Mountain State, as management took some time coming up with a solution beyond the anticipatorily intentionally large outfield. A humidor was ultimately installed on the premises to store balls, in order to keep them slightly more pliable than they would be sitting out in dryness, and thus, a little harder to drive over the fence. At the end of the day, however, nothing can be done for the thin air itself, and a trip to Coors Field might afford a wonderful day of hitters' baseball for fans. Eric Young was the first player to hit a home run at Coors, and he did it at the very first at bat! Incidentally, Dante Bichette, the Jupiter player we mentioned in the first chapter, was the first player to hit a home run in Rockies' history, in 1993. He was part of a group of players collectively known as the Blake Street Bombers, after their tendency to hit the ball out of the park, along with Larry Walker, Vinny Castilla, Andrés Galarraga, and a few others. These home runs are something that every Rockies fan remembers. Grant was very excited to meet Eric Young, now first base coach for the Colorado Rockies, at spring training this past year when he was bat boy. Eric Young Jr., his son, plays for the Brewers.

Coors Field is an interesting mix of unique and classic baseball stadium aesthetics. It definitely follows the school of neoclassical stadium design. Drawing off the classics like Wrigley Field, Fenway Park, and the long-mourned Ebbets Field that put an emphasis on regal, red-brick pillars set against the structure's main face, neoclassical (or retro) baseball park design began with Oriole Park at Camden Yards in 1992, and has been followed by many other newer stadiums, including Globe Life Park in Arlington, Citi Field, and Turner Field. At the same time, Coors Field is very isolated, and opens up to the almost impossibly wide Rocky Mountain sky.

The East Coast boasts quite a few stadiums, some very close to each other. Yankee Stadium and Citi Field in New York, for example, are less than ten miles apart. Coors, on the other hand, is nearly six hundred miles away from Kauffman Stadium in Kansas City, the next closest MLB venue! Don't let its location dissuade you from catching a game, however. Coors offers some of the most affordable tickets in the business, with seating in the "Rockpile" (the deep center bleacher section) starting off at four dollars for most games if bought a few days in advance. Given its out-of-the-way location for most folks and high elevation, visiting Coors Field provides a very unique experience.

You may have noticed that the unique features of certain ballparks lend them to favoring hitters or pitchers. This is a very frequently made distinction in baseball, and in recent years our own Petco Park often topped the list of "pitchers' parks." In fact, it was so hard to hit a home run at Petco for so many years that in 2012, management made some major modifications to the outfield, and brought the fences in. The outfield was reduced in size by about a dozen feet as a result, and the right field wall was lowered a few feet. Overall the changes seem to have been effective, and we have been seeing a few more home runs over the past few seasons! There's no set, definitive way to measure which parks are pitcher's parks and which are hitter's parks (although baseball fanatics will sure spend a lot of time arguing about it!). There are always going to be players who come along and have games perfectly adapted to the fields and make them produce very unusual results. Here are some of the parks that have interesting structures and factors that generally skew them towards one of these two categories:

Hitters' Parks	Pitchers' Parks
Coors: A hitting mecca because of the high altitude and lower atmosphere, the team estimates that a ball hit here can travel 9% further than one hit at sea-level. The altitude also affects pitchers negatively, as the thinner air decreases resistance.	**Safeco:** Long considered one of baseball's most extreme pitchers' parks, it features a large outfield and extra deep center field that makes hitting the ball out of the field very difficult.
Globe Life in Arlington: Low humidity and year-round warm temperatures, along with swirling wind gusts that help fly balls over the outfield walls combine with short fences and a lack of foul territory to make this park a real winner for hitters.	**AT&T:** The humid summers and winds that come off the bay right outside keep balls in the park. Along with the large outfield and extra deep center field, these factors highly benefit pitchers.
Chase: Dry, thin desert air, combined with particularly low walls and flatter angles in the outfield that make a larger swath of grass for outfielders to cover, make for many great home runs.	**Petco:** Designed with the most spacious outfield in the MLB--so extreme that it was reconfigured before the 2013 season, with the walls being brought in ten feet and lowered by two feet, to try and start leveling the playing field.
Rogers: The AstroTurf makes balls bounce high and at weird angles, which messes with defensive plays. It's also is one of the more rare symmetrical ballparks, with porches in reach down the lines, so hitters from both sides of the plate are at advantage.	**Dodger:** Walls are higher than most MLB fields for this subterranean stadium, and center field is very deep, with the highest pitching mound in the MLB, which allows pitchers to get under the ball more effectively.
Great American: Smaller dimensions, with a shallow center field, and right field walls that are only eight feet high, make hitting a ball out of the park here much easier.	**PNC:** The summer high temperatures, intense humidity from the river, high wall in right field, and spacious left field make this park one of the most pitcher friendly.

Of course, the stadiums offer different game day mechanics for the fans, as well! Making a dive to snag a foul or home run ball is a time-honored tradition for the fans, and you will see them scrambling at every game to get these mementos. At AT&T Park in San Francisco, however, the particularly adventurous gather in kayaks on the Bay itself, off the right field wall, in the hopes that some talented lefty will send a ball their way. They come equipped with nets of all sizes, jostling for position. The occasional fan, not fearing the chilly West Coast water, has been known to dive right in! This area, though officially known as the China Basin, is called McCovey Cove by fans, in honor of the retired Giants player Willie McCovey. It is fitting that a hard-to-hit area would be named after McCovey, as he was known during his career to be one of the strongest active hitters, capable of sending home runs soaring over 450 feet through the air. Over 2500 miles away, strong hitters can find another aquatic target in the form of the Allegheny River, which runs alongside PNC Park in Pittsburgh for a portion of the right field fence. It takes quite a bit more power to hit one over the multi-leveled stands there, but boat owners should beware when certain players are in town! The bodies of water close to both PNC and Great American Ballpark have the reputation for kicking up winds, breezes, and sudden gusts that can also affect the play of a traveling ball.

Stadiums also vary when it comes to fan enthusiasm, a factor that can in turn affect the players. The Cardinals fans at Busch Stadium and Red Sox fans at Fenway are always incredibly passionate, and stood out to us as some of the most loyal and appreciative in the league. Both St. Louis and Boston have deep baseball traditions, and their clubs have won eleven and eight World Series championships, respectively, over the past hundred years. Couple this with the fact that both stadiums are on the smaller side, and you have a recipe for frequently sold out games, loud crowds, and a consistently high energy level.

Fan enthusiasm can cut both ways. Over the course of our trip, we made it to one opening day game, and it was a truly amazing experience. The game was the Texas Rangers opener against the Angels in 2013 at Globe Life Park in Arlington, Texas. The opening ceremony was pretty incredible, particularly the unfurling of a massive American flag across nearly the entire outfield by men and women from every branch of the armed services. As the flag grew to cover the pristine field, the National Anthem was sung by Jack Ingram, and six World War II era planes flew overhead. It was a pleasant, beautiful day, and the entire ceremony gave us chills.

The Texas Rangers are also known for having high attendance and eager home crowds, and opening day was no exception. The game was completely sold out, and the fans were eager to get the ball rolling on another Rangers season. There were some disgruntled fans in attendance, though, as it was the first return game for MVP and Home Run Derby star Josh Hamilton, who was playing for the Angels against Texas for the first time, after five seasons with the Rangers. He was booed each time he stepped up to the plate, and some fans even whipped out newspapers and pretended to completely ignore him. It definitely affected his play a bit, and he struck out during his first at-bat in just four pitches. He would strike out once more and remain hitless over the course of this uncomfortable reunion, and later admitted that it messed with his ability to play the game. Just as a loyal and energetic crowd can prop up the home team, they can discourage the opponents as well! All ends well here, though, as Hamilton ended up back on the Rangers during the 2015 season, and after a standing ovation from the home crowd, hit a vicious double on the first pitch of his first at-bat.

In any event, the rest of the opening day game in Arlington was a crowd pleaser. During pre-game batting practice, Albert Pujols of the Angels hit a ball over the fence during batting practice, and one of the Angels' coaches gave Jack and Grant the ball after they went nuts displaying their traveling Rally Monkey, yelling, "Rally Monkey!" The Angels took an early lead in the second, but the Rangers didn't take long to rally for themselves, as A.J. Pierzynski hit a picture-perfect triple down the right field foul line during the next inning that batted in a run. The Rangers later scored in the fifth inning as well, taking the lead. Los Angeles struck back in the seventh to tie the game back up, setting the stage for a game-winning home run from Adrián Beltré. Beltré is a known slugger, and has hit so many home runs that his teammates pretend to fall asleep in the dugout after each one! There were over 48,000 spectators during this game, definitely the largest crowd we have been a part of, and the roar they gave an opening day, game-winning home run was bound to be deafening! Joe Nathan, the closer, took to the mound in the ninth and kept the

Angels at bay, protecting the Rangers' one-run lead. In doing so, Nathan achieved his 299th career save, and the Rangers started off their season with a bang. The boys remembered this fine performance some time later when Nathan signed a ball for them during a visiting game at Petco.

The Rangers have some great Texan traditions that the already-exuberant crowd loves to get behind. Dancing cowgirls on the dugouts during the seventh-inning stretch danced a do-si-do to country music, and the whole crowd joined in singing "Deep in the Heart of Texas" during the fifth. Our first opening day game was a resounding success, and we really wish we had been able to attend more. Maybe a tour of every teams' opening day celebrations will be the topic of our next book! In any event, we finished off the trip with a great meal at an authentic, award-winning Texan steakhouse, the Saltgrass, and went on with our journey.

Wrigley, the Chicago Cubs' park, is the second-oldest stadium in major league baseball, and it houses an extremely dedicated fan base—some would say even more so than the Rangers. While the Rangers' fans booed a former player on his return game for a different team, the Cubs fans took team loyalty even further! We saw two games at Wrigley in 2013, and in the first, Pedro Álvarez hit a home run for the visiting team, the Pirates. You have probably pieced together that this would be a great prize for most baseball fans, particularly young fans like Grant and Jack. Not so at Wrigley. This home run put the Pirates in the lead, which was frustrating enough. Add this to the fact that the Cubs were in something of a multi-year slump, and the fans were downright incensed. Once they managed to get a hold of the ball, they threw it right back into the outfield in defiance! They would end the day much happier, as Alfonso Soriano would end up hitting two-run homers in back-to-back innings immediately afterwards, and the Cubs would coast to a 4-1 victory. Never underestimate fandoms that run generations deep!

Things aren't always so pleasant for the home crowd, and teams in the middle of a poor season will definitely have less lively crowds. It is very easy to tell when the energy is low, and when that is taking a toll on the players' abilities to compete. This is a bit of a mixed experience; on the one hand, a string of poor performances means games won't be sold out, and tickets will be easy and cheap to get. On the other hand, nothing is worse than a low-energy ballgame! We have a friend at the Oakland A's who has been working behind the scenes with the team for seventeen years in guest services. She was wondering how the announcers went through these ups and downs every day, getting to the game and staying excited, and received a great answer from Ray Fosse, broadcaster for Oakland. He said, "Yes, baseball can be slow, and if the home team hasn't been doing very well, it can be a long day! But you can come to the ballpark every day knowing that something is going to make you smile. You can always stay positive, because you know that looking out into the field, something special will happen. There will always be at least one good thing to happen that day, be it a triple play, home run, or diving catch." After she told us this, we did look at the game differently the next day. Keep your eye on the ball, and you will see something that turns an ordinary game into something special! Anything can happen, and the course of a game can change suddenly, off the momentum of a home run or a steal.

The other MLB stadium in Texas is Minute Maid Park in Houston, which we visited the very next day. Minute Maid is pretty new, and is interesting because it has gone by several names since it opened in 2000. Initially it was known as Enron Field, as the naming rights had been bought by the tech giant. After the infamous collapse of Enron and its bankruptcy filing in 2001, the Astros bought back the naming rights from the company. The park was known simply as Astros Field for a period of time. It was named once again, this time in a nod to the city's history, as The Ballpark at Union Station. One hundred years ago, Houston was one of the most important railway cities in the country, and its main structure was Union Station. Along the left field edge of the stadium is a miniature train, which moves back and forth after an Astro home run or win, in another nod to the city's past. Finally, in 2002, the Coca-Cola Company picked up the naming rights, and Minute Maid Park was born again.

The game started off slow, with no runs scored in the first three innings. Things started to heat up right away though, as the visiting

Oakland Athletics would take the lead in the fourth by a score of 3 to 1. A few innings later, and the game had turned into a home run fest! Crisp, Smith, and Lowrie all hit home runs for the A's and won the game 6 to 3. In fact, Lowrie and Smith's homers were both on the first pitch of their at-bats, which was pretty wild. Not to be outdone, Jason Castro hit a home run for the Astros, which meant that we got to see the train in action. All told, it was a great day for baseball action, meeting players, and getting autographs. It was a great baseball day in almost every way!

CHAPTER FOUR

No Autographs Please

The activity of autograph hunting is an acquired skill. In this chapter we hope to impart some well-earned tips for starting your own collection of signed baseball paraphernalia. It isn't easy, but it is a great deal of fun!

We are big fans of Miller Park. Spending time there is wonderful, a completely unique baseball experience. We attended two games on back-to-back nights there in 2013, and saw some fantastic baseball. The first game was between the Brewers and the Mets. Before we had even found our seats, we were walking through the park, taking in the sights and trying to decide what to grab to eat, when the boys stopped in their tracks. They had recognized famous baseball announcer and comedian Bob Uecker's voice from hearing it on TV! They were very excited about hearing him. Most baseball fans will remember his famous line, "Just a bit outside," from the classic comedy *Major League.* The boys had gotten a hard-won and highly treasured Matt Harvey autograph, along with signatures from several other players that day. On the second day, we got to fit in some activities that we had missed the evening before, like trying our luck in the pitching zone, where a speedometer tells you how your throw stacks up against the pros. Jack and Grant acquitted themselves well, throwing fastballs at 45 and 51 mph, respectively!

The opening pitch to the game involved a little more fanfare than we usually see. A few years beforehand, Miller Park had struck an advertising deal with Harley-Davidson, giving the motorcycle company a branded, newly constructed seating area in the upper levels. If you happen to be in the Harley Owners Group heading to Miller Park, make sure to check it out before ordering your tickets…you'll get a discount on both regular and post-season games! One other stipulation of the deal was that the ball for every opening pitch was to be delivered to the home plate umpire by a rider on a Harley motorcycle. We were a bit surprised to see a sharply-dressed motorist drive through the right field foul territory to ramp up the crowd and hand off the ball. It was definitely a crowd-pleaser, and got everyone in the mood to watch an exciting game!

Miller Park is another more modern stadium. It opened in 2001, and is a significant architectural achievement. It has a retractable dome roof, the only fan-shaped one in the country, featuring massive glass panes that flood the stadium with natural light, even when the roof is closed. We had the chance to see the dome close, which is accomplished in a mere seven minutes. When the roof is retracted, the stadium has a stunning profile best viewed from across the main parking area, with the glass and metal structure rising up over three hundred feet into the air. Almost any view of the stadium from the outside is impressive. When the roof is closed, the best view is looking up from the front entrance, as the handsome red brick façade is capped off by a star-shaped ridge where the two moving portions meet.

Like several other stadiums along the way, Miller Park features some interesting statues. Some of the first of these that visitors see are in front of the main entrance to the stadium, and depict Robin Yount, who spent his entire twenty-year career playing for the Brewers, and the legendary Hank Aaron. Hank Aaron ruled the home run charts for more than a quarter of a century, and his career 755 homers stood atop the charts until he was overtaken in 2007 by Barry Bonds. The Brewers take great pride in the history of their team, and also commemorate important players in the club's past in the Walk of Fame, located outside the stadium. You will find both Yount and Aaron featured again on the walk, along with fifteen other players, owners, and broadcasters associated with the team. Each is remembered by a home plate-shaped plaque featuring the honoree's name, signature, and dates they were with the club. The plaques are set in the same red brick that is used throughout the rest of the stadium, and offer an historic and beautiful attraction for those interested in the history of the game.

The most prominent statue, however, is a larger-than-life depiction of "Bud" Selig, Commissioner of Baseball for MLB and former owner of the Brewers. In the 1960s and 1970s, Selig was instrumental in keeping major league baseball in Milwaukee, and in 1970 he purchased the Seattle Pilots and moved them to his town, where they remain the Brewers to this day. Selig is one of the most influential figures in Brewers' and MLB history, and his tireless effort to support major league play in the Milwaukee area is justly honored by this beautiful statue.

Inside the stadium, one will find the *Teamwork* sculpture, which was installed in 2001 in memory of three workers who perished in an accident during the construction of the stadium's dome. It is a beautiful and sad memorial, and we are incredibly thankful for their sacrifice. The stadium is their legacy, and will stand for decades to come as a testament to their ingenuity, creativity, and building prowess.

The food at Miller Park is among the best in the business. While Jack and Grant feasted on excellent nachos and hot dogs, the rest of us had carved turkey sandwiches in section 222. The turkey is smoked on-site, and sliced up right then and there before being turned into a sandwich. It was fresh and delicious, and if we were forced to list our favorite foods of the tour, these sandwiches would definitely be towards the top!

Miller Park is committed to providing a variety of activities for fans of all levels and ages. The stadium features a wide array of additional features that appeal to kids and adults alike. After games on Sundays, kids under sixteen are allowed to run the bases. As one of our rules is to arrive early and stay late, giving it a try was an easy decision for Grant and Jack! During games, Bernie's Clubhouse offers younger children a place to play interactive games and snack on kid-specific concessions.

Miller Park definitely had some of the largest crowds and lines of our trip. There was a giveaway, where fans could get a bobblehead of Hank Aaron. We faced the crowd, and couldn't believe how long the line was!

The stadium also has some of the most extensive parking we've seen—sixteen parking lots, with a total of 12,000 spaces! It has become tradition for many fans to tailgate before the game, weather permitting. This is definitely a practice more commonly seen before football games, but the Milwaukee crowd is a committed bunch!

The fans at Miller Park are always great, and the stadium offers a number of fun traditions to make the most of this. One of these is a mascot race featuring sausages that takes place before the seventh inning. The Famous Racing Sausages are comprised of a bratwurst, an Italian sausage, a Polish sausage, a hot dog, and a chorizo. The first four began racing in the 90s, and moved with the rest of the team to Miller Park in 2001, where they were joined by the chorizo. They race every game, from deep left field to home plate, and are always a hit. The players get just as excited as the crowds, and often root loudly for their favorites. Some players have even slipped into a costume at the end of the sixth inning in order to race as one of their edible heroes! The Sausages are no slouches when it comes to record-keeping, befitting mascots in a sport like baseball, and the standings are a closely watched statistic on the Brewers' website. Once a year, when the Pirates play the Brewers, there is a race between the Pittsburgh Pierogies and the Sausages that rivals the intensity of any playoff game. Together with the racing Presidents of Nationals Park, these teams make up a league of their own. And, just like the Presidents, they have seen their own share of drama! In 2013, the Italian sausage was actually kidnapped! After a few days of partying, dancing, and more, the costume was returned unharmed, but not without plenty of pictures and video to prove it!

All of the Brewers' mascots love having their picture taken, and we got some with the Polish sausage, Italian Sausage, Chorizo, and Bernie (the official mascot) himself. If you are planning to hit any of these stadiums and your schedule is flexible, it would be worth your time to see a race!

No visit to Miller Park is complete without a quick trip down Bernie Brewer's Slide. The Brewers have always been highly focused on the fan experience, a tradition that can be traced back to an early, particularly dedicated fan by the name of Milt Mason. During the 1970 season, the

Brewers were struggling, and in order to attract viewers to the stadium (at that time, Milwaukee County Stadium), he stayed on top of the scoreboard for forty days. Other fans brought him food, and when the Brewers finally scored a victory over the Indians, he slid down on a rope before 44,000 cheering fans. Bernie Brewer the mascot is a smiling man in Mason's image, with a huge mustache, who leads the Milwaukee crowd from his own dugout above left field at Miller Park. In honor of Mason, whenever the home team hits a home run, he rockets down his yellow slide to land onto a giant home plate. Fans can also take a trip down the slide, but if you want to, you will have to schedule it before the game. Luckily, booking tickets for the slide includes a behind-the-scenes tour of the stadium, which was fantastic.

At the point in the season that we attended games at Miller Park, the Brewers weren't doing particularly well, and found themselves at the bottom of the NL Central Division. During the first game we attended, the Brewers suffered a discouraging loss to the New York Mets by a score of 2 to 1. Despite catcher Jonathan Lucroy hitting his tenth home run of the year for Milwaukee in the seventh inning, the home team was unable to mount a comeback and tallied up another loss. As usual, we were rooting for the home team, and we were particularly bummed because the Brewers fans were so full of hometown spirit!

We weren't optimistic in the chances for the game the next day. The Reds were doing much better than the Brewers, and were still helmed by Cincinnati's no-hitter hero, Homer Bailey. Despite their poor season, the Brewers still had every intention of putting on a good performance, and ultimately gave the home crowd plenty to cheer about. Lucroy hit a nice home run to give Milwaukee the lead, and they went into the ninth inning leading by a run.

At the top of the ninth, Joey Votto, the defensive savior of the no-hitter, took the plate. There were two outs, and the Reds had a player on first. Rodriguez threw a blistering, ninety mile-per-hour fastball right over the middle of the plate, and Votto connected. He definitely hit it hard enough to send it over the fence for what should have been a game-winning home run, but he also got under it quite a bit. This gave the ball's trajectory a very high curve, which allowed Carlos Gomez, the Brewers center fielder and future Golden Glove winner, to keep his eye on it as he sprinted for the fence. Once there, he stutter-stepped for a split second to gauge the ball's path, then made a perfectly timed leap. He stretched out his glove over the top of the eight-foot fence and snagged the ball at the last second, ending the game instantly. The expressions on his teammates' faces changed from frustration at the apparently winning hit, to uncertainty at what had just happened at the center field fence, to elation in victory over the course of a few seconds, as the triumphant Gomez ran back to the infield. For a second, Votto himself wasn't sure what he had seen, but the fans had gotten an up close and personal view. The catch was replayed on ESPN for the rest of the night, and we were happy to watch it again back at our hotel room!

We did have one harrowing experience at Miller Park. One of the ever-present concerns when looking to get an autograph, particularly when kids are involved, is the crowd. When we were at the Brewers versus Mets game, we had the chance beforehand to get an autograph from Matt Harvey, pitcher for New York. Jack, always on the lookout, was the first one to spot him nearby during the warmup, and told the rest of us, "Hey! That's Matt Harvey!" Dayna leaned over slowly and whispered, "Who is Matt Harvey?" Incredulous, Jack quickly gave her the run-down of his stats, facts, and figures for the year! He was bewildered that she didn't know who he was. Matt had actually just been named to the NL All-Star Team, and was in the middle of an outstanding season. He was quite popular, and the home crowd was eager to meet him and get his autograph.

Jack politely called him over to the stands during the warm-up, and when Matt was done he came right over to the boys. Before he started walking over, we were mostly alone, but as he started over, it only took a few seconds for a *sea* of people to descend on the area, all jostling for position! We were swarmed! It was a little scary for a few moments, and Dayna kept calling out to the boys to make sure they were all right as they got sucked into the crowd. There was no need to worry in the end, as by that point, Jack and Grant were seasoned pros themselves at negotiating the crowds at a ballgame. They were even able to get the autographs! It is definitely a good idea to assume that there will be crowds in situations like this, and to be ready if you lose sight of friends or family.

From the very beginning, when Jack and Grant first suggested that we travel as a family to all of the MLB stadiums, one of the things they wanted to focus on during the trips was collecting souvenirs and mementos of the journey. Of course, all the stadiums have stores that supply fans with a wide variety of gear to choose from, and over the course of completing our adventure, we have collected hats, jerseys, cards, and more. None of these goods, however, has the emotional and personal touch that an autograph does, especially if you have a great story about worming your way through the crowd to get it! Becoming accomplished autograph hunters wasn't easy, and our approach developed over time as we learned what to do and what not to do. We're here to share our hard-earned tips and tricks, so that you can start your own collection, or improve on an existing one!

The first priority when preparing to get autographs is to have your equipment in order. Baseball offers one pretty obvious vehicle for your autograph collection: baseballs! We started off using basic and inexpensive balls that can be bought in bulk at any department or sports store, but found that, in the long run, it is best to invest in some genuine, high-quality MLB balls. They are somewhat more expensive, but they will last the longest, and the autograph will remain pristine and legible for years and years. We've made a habit of keeping one or two in our pockets while out and about in the stadium, as you never know when the opportunity will arise to get a solo autograph. We've managed to get autographs from several retired Hall of Famers this way, including Manny Sanguillén. This is a practice that we're considering extending to trips around town between games. We were incredibly lucky on one of our trips to New York, and ended bumping into Joe Girardi, Yankees manager, in Central Park! Next time, we will definitely have a ball for him to sign. Remember, even if you have multiple items on you, try not to ask a player to sign more than one; not only does it make it seem like you might be looking to sell their autographs, but it shows a lack of respect for the courtesy that they are giving you.

As far as writing utensils are concerned, stick with high-quality ballpoint pens instead of Sharpies for balls. Sharpies tend to bleed into the leather a bit over time, and if you get drenched, like we did the day before Bailey's no-hitter, you might have some ruined signatures! Most autograph aficionados agree that blue ink shows up much nicer on a new ball than black, but the functional difference is minimal. Occasionally forgers will try to print out a signature and paste it onto a ball to sell, so in some circles blue ink is preferred over black because it precludes this kind of trickery and shows the autograph is genuine. If you are planning on keeping your autographed balls, either will do fine.

There is a place on both baseballs and bats called the "sweet spot." This area allows for the largest transferal of force between two objects— so hitting a baseball on the sweet spot will send it farther and higher, and hitting it with the sweet spot of the bat will add even more power to the hit. On baseball bats, the sweet spot is usually a few inches before the tip. When the sweet spot of a bat hits a ball, vibrations are kept to a minimum and the full force of the swing is exerted on the ball. On the ball itself, the sweet spot is located at the bottom of the horseshoe formed by the stitches. This area is usually the best place to get a ball signed. For one thing, it gives the most space to write, so players with long signatures won't get cramped trying to write there. It also offers a clean, legible view of the signature, and you won't be able to see logos along with the script. When a team is signing a ball, the sweet spot is usually reserved for the manager of the team, or some other figure central to the leadership of the club. If you are at a scheduled signing, players will often sign the sweet spot automatically, unless many other signing players are present. Some players won't sign on the sweet spot right away, either out of personal preference or because they think the ball will be sold. At unscheduled signings during warmups or at spring training, plays might sign anywhere on the ball and you might have to ask them to sign the sweet spot. They have a lot going on and might need to rush right back to the field. It is safe to assume that a kid isn't going to sell the ball, though, and many of the players we asked signed the sweet spot without additional requests. If you have a kid asking for the autograph, it is generally fine for them to ask the player to sign on the sweet spot. Adults asking might give the impression that they are trying to sell the ball, and get turned down.

Over the years, we have slowly been adding baseball bats to our collection as well, and we plan on adding more in the future. They offer a few distinct advantages and disadvantages over balls and other small items. On the plus side, they have more signage space, which means they are perfect for team signings. Unfortunately, you can't bring baseball bats into almost any of the MLB stadiums on regular days, as they usually fall under the "No Weapons" rules of the venue. Oakland Coliseum, also known as the home of the A's, is the only park we are aware of that lets fans bring bats to sign at every game, which made it one of the most accessible parks on our trip. Just make sure to check it in at the service counter after the National Anthem. We're always on the lookout for "Bat Day" themed games, where teams will hand out bats as a promotion and you can get them signed. Bringing your own bats is a great way to get autographs at other events, though, and we have gotten plenty of them signed at spring training. Make sure you stock up beforehand! After getting to the Phoenix area for spring training a few years ago, we had to run around from store to store looking for bats, as we found out that we weren't the first to have this idea. Bats are a great way to collect autographs, they just require a little more planning!

Wooden bats are the way to go for autographs. Our signed bats are pretty basic, solid maple or ash Louisville Sluggers in a natural finish, which can be found at any sporting goods store. You will find much more variety in preferences and recommendations in the autograph world for writing tools, and ink colors for bats, but we tend to prefer the classic black or blue Sharpie on our light-colored bats. Wooden bats are less porous than leather baseballs, so you don't have to worry as much about the ink bleeding; we recommend Sharpies for bat autographs, since ballpoint pens can be more difficult to get a legible signature onto the wood. Others prefer darker bats with silver paint pens, but we haven't given that a shot yet!

One of the best spots we've found for getting bats signed is at spring training camps. They do have different layouts and can be very large, but you will have a great time if you are looking for autographs. The Peoria Sports Complex in Phoenix, Arizona, which services our Padres and the Seattle Mariners, is great for autograph hunters during exhibition games, for example. The training areas for minor league players are off to the left side once you go through the main entrance, and it is very easy to approach players there. The major guys are to the right side, and they are generally very easy to approach as well. So, if you plan on incorporating Peoria into a spring training tour, wear some nice walking shoes. It is definitely worth it! The Tempe Diablo Stadium (also in Arizona) is another great place to grab some autographs. This is where the Los Angeles Angels of Anaheim train, and they tend to always having batting practice on the field, where the players are easily accessible to the fans. Some major league teams practice at different locations than their minor league counterparts, however. For example, the Oakland A's train at Hohokam Stadium, but their minor league players play at Fitch Park which is a few blocks away. There are plenty of combinations of teams, practices, and parks during spring training, so do your research and plan ahead if your goal is to get some gear signed!

There are plenty of other things that make for great keepsakes when autographed, like batting helmets or gloves. Lots of fans bring gloves to games anyway, in the hopes of snagging a foul or home run ball. The boys always did this, even from the start of our journey. They were never without their gloves, so that even when we weren't at a game hoping for a foul ball, they were playing catch. Eventually they said to Dayna, "Mom, you should get your own glove, so we can play catch!" Dayna thought that was a good idea, and got a Rawlings glove with pink leather! Our friend Bud Black, whom you will meet later, signed it on Mother's Day some years ago, when the boys took her to a game. For darker items like gloves (that are *not* pink!), a silver paint pen works best. There will be no bleeding, and the contrast will make for a crisp, clear autograph. Silver paint pens work great for getting autographs on photographs and the darker parts of baseball cards as well.

It can be helpful to come up with autograph goals before even arriving at a game, and equipping yourself appropriately. You can only bring so much with you into a baseball game, so decide if you want to try and get balls, cards, photos, or a glove signed. Bring the pen or Sharpie that will work best for those items, and then throw in a few extras. You don't want to get to the front of the crowd and make contact with the player only for the pen to be busted, and not have a replacement. It is also wise to test your pens beforehand to make sure they are in good working order!

Before heading to a game, look up a few key athletes that will be playing, and make a note of their recent statistics or accomplishments. It is always nice to have something individually specific to say while chatting with a signing player, so that you can cap off the experience with that personal touch. Lots of players prefer to give autographs to kids, since they tend to be more openly grateful and excited, and no doubt the players themselves remember being baseball-loving youngsters. Occasionally, Jack and Grant will get a bit flustered or overexcited at this stage during a signing; that's why Dad is there to swoop in and congratulate the player on a certain play from earlier in the season, or offer commiseration on a near miss.

Don't unnecessarily interrupt a player or manager, and try not to monopolize their signing time at the expense of other fans when you do have their attention. Many times, managers and players invite their own friends and family to the game. It is pretty normal for these guests to yell down to the dugout and get the player's attention, so that they can chat for a minute before and after the game. You can certainly tell when a player is trying to have a conversation with family members or friends, and these are the worst times to ask for an autograph. Just pay attention, and it will become obvious.

For example, when we were at spring training, we were having a conversation with at the time Padres' bench coach Dave Roberts after the game. At the time we were writing this book, Roberts had just been named manager of the Los Angeles Dodgers. He is a something of local hero, from Rancho Buena Vista High School, and Dayna had yelled hello to him, saying "Hi coach, greetings from La Costa Valley," and he had been kind enough to come over and chat. We are huge fans of Roberts, and will always remember his legendary steal while playing for the Red Sox against the New York Yankees in the 2004 AL Championship. The Red Sox were facing elimination, having lost the first three games. Famed NY closer Mariano Rivera was called to the mound with the Yankees leading 4 to 3, and he walked Kevin Millar. Roberts, known for his incredible speed and wits for base running, was called in to replace Millar at first as a pinch runner. After a brilliant game of cat and mouse with Rivera (who checked him not once, not twice, but three times), Roberts successfully stole second base. Then, Bill Mueller hit a line-drive single right down center field. Roberts, from second base, went all the way home, tying the game. After going into extra innings, the Red Sox would win an incredible eight games in a row, winning the World Series. If Roberts hadn't employed his great speed and performed "The Steal of the Century," that single might not have scored a run, and the series might have ended very differently.

In any event, we were thrilled to get to talk to Roberts. He is an immensely nice guy, and is co-owner of Red Stitch Wine, which we really enjoy as well. One or two fans came over and were a bit pushy about getting autographs, so he said, "I'd be happy to sign for you, after my conversation with some friends." As usual, common sense and good manners are your best guides! It's always a good practice to let players have their space, and wait patiently and quietly for the player or coach to finish their conversation. After all, the experience isn't just about getting the thing you wanted, it is about building goodwill and rapport with the players. We are all in the stadium because we share a love of the game, and everyone should come away from a signing feeling like they've been part of something special and cool!

When you attend a lot of games, you will experience a wide array of responses from players when you're trying to meet them or acquire autographs. Be prepared to be ignored or turned down, particularly if you find yourself surrounded by an overly boisterous or pushy crowd. In fact, one of the most memorable and worthwhile games we attended, the Homer Bailey no-hitter, started out as quite the dud in this regard. We had settled in initially on the visitor side, in our visitor gear, hoping to get some balls from the practicing outfielders. This is usually a pretty successful tactic, as pursuing the visiting team means you won't be in competition with the (sometimes upwards of thirty-thousand!) home fans hunting for autographs and balls of their own. Players on the road also appreciate seeing a friendly face! Dressing the part, and showing your enthusiasm for baseball and team colors is important, and the players love seeing fans in their shirts and jerseys before an away game—it can give them a real boost! In this case, however, the Giants were very focused on their warmup, and it was all business that particular day. Suffice to say we struck out on getting any interaction or autographs from the visiting Giants. We learned a few lessons about being baseball fans that day. On the one hand, you can expect to be disappointed every once in a while. On the other, one of the joys of the game is that it can always surprise you!

Persistence can sometimes be key! Kris Bryant, currently playing third base for the Chicago Cubs, attended the University of San Diego, and was one of the most talked about rookies of the 2015 season. One of his first games after being called up in 2015 was at Petco Park back in San Diego, and we were there. At one point before the game he was available for autographs, and he was absolutely swamped by fans, both kids and adults alike. It quickly turned into a roving mob of eager fans hoping to get an autograph, and Grant disappeared into the fray. We were a bit worried, since he had just gotten his arm out of a cast earlier that day, but he eventually emerged out of the melee gripping his trophy, a signed ball. He had never stopped trying, and the ball is now a prized part of his collection.

Sometimes, you will just get lucky. We had seen Andrew McCutchen play several times in other games, at a number of different stadiums and we had never gotten his autograph. As an MVP and five-time All-Star for the Pittsburgh Pirates, he is always fantastic to watch. Anyway, we had been at Busch Stadium getting autographs before the Cardinals game against the Pirates, and Grant had gathered three Pirate players' signatures on his ball. Grant got up to go to the restroom, and left the signed ball in his cup holder. When he came back to his seat, the ball was gone! You can imagine his disappointment to find that his autographed ball was missing. After this mishap, a few moments later Grant was taking in the sights on the field, still feeling bummed about the ball, when suddenly McCutchen started walking back towards the dugout after warmups. Grant immediately sprang into action and ran over with Jack. Steve, who was several rows up watching everything, had even turned to another man in the crowd and laughingly bet that he wouldn't stop and sign. To our surprise, and delight, McCutchen came right over to the boys! Grant whipped out the extra ball he kept in his pocket and they both got signatures. Wow, what a rollercoaster of excitement! The baseball angels were looking over the boys that day!

They were very happy with the prized and coveted autograph, to say the least, and have been big fans of the legendary McCutchen ever since. We were glad a year later to see him at our own Petco, and we got his autograph again. This was after the championship game featuring Jack's rec ball team, the Pirates. After our game the team went down to Petco, all dressed in Pirates' gear. We were behind the dugout watching the warm up, and McCutchen actually came over to sign for the whole team. We also got to meet Clint Hurdle, manager for the Pirates, and Jordy Mercer, second baseman, who gave his bat to one of the boys on the team. Even though it all worked out in this case, there is another lesson: we would have loved to meet and get autographs from countless players, like Derek Jeter, Mike Trout, and the list goes on, but you will never be able to get them all. Do the best you can, like the players themselves, and watch your collection grow!

Learn to temper your expectations for autographs, especially if you are in it for fun, like we are, and aren't plan on selling your collection. You won't always be able to meet the player you had planned on meeting, or get that coveted autograph. You are going to have good and bad experiences. One night you might be skunked, the next night you might get one signature, and the third night you might get many balls tossed to you from the outfield during warmup. Win or lose, you will learn a lot, and will be better prepared for next time.

Remember to look out for the fans around you; as wonderful as it is to build your own collection, some of the best autograph memories Grant and Jack have are of helping others. The boys have the habit now of spreading their luck to those around them. If they had a good day and collected some balls, like we did at Safeco, they will give an extra to a kid without one. The boys are eager to help other kids get a ball. Another thing we like to do is carry around a few extra packs of baseball cards, to share with kids who maybe missed out on snagging a home run or foul ball. It's great karma, and it's wonderful watching our boys trying to pay it forward.

As a family, we had a lot of fun coming up with interesting, unique, or funny ways to get the players' attentions during warm ups. Bright blue and green wigs, the Yoda doll, and the Rally Monkey all worked well, but homemade signs really seemed to turn heads. They are easy to read from a distance, and a clever sign will create an immediate impact. They have also gotten us a few cameos on the Jumbotron and television. They are very simple to make— our technique just involves taping two pieces of cardboard together and coming up with something unique to say. As great as it is catching the attention of cameras, a huge advantage we have over others in the stadium is that they sometimes forget that the players want to be entertained and appreciated too. When we are making a sign at home, we are actually coming up with ways to talk to the players directly. Signs can be the best way to make a player laugh. After all, despite loving what they do, the players are also doing their jobs, and a moment of levity can really make all the difference in their days.

In 2013, when the Pirates were having a great season, we made a sign that read, "This is Arrrgh Year," complete with skull and crossbones! We brought it to the Pirates versus Cubs game at Wrigley Field, and it was a hit. At the opening of the Padres 2015 season, another example of a creative sign the boys made highlighted that there were four Wills playing for the team—Will Venable, Wil Myers, Will Middlebrooks, and Wil Nieves. Interestingly, Nieves would hit a grand slam in the fourth inning. The sign was entitled, "Where there's a Will, there's a Padre!" The Wills who saw it loved it, and we got three of the four to autograph it. Another Will that we added to the sign was Will Ferrell.

Ferrell did a really neat video special during spring training, where he played all nine positions for a little bit during exhibition games. It was meant to raise money for a charity he works closely with, Cancer for College. In the video, he is traded and cut in comical fashion from all the teams, and it was wildly popular with baseball fans across the nation. During this "Ferrell Takes the Field" HBO special, baseball cards were made for Will, depicting him on each of the ten teams he went through during spring training. He so-called "retired" with the Padres, so we made a blown-up version of his San Diego card with the caption, "HALL OF FAMER???" We were also lucky enough to have been extras in *Anchorman 2*, filmed in our hometown of San Diego. We think very highly of him and his charity, and it is great that he is a fellow baseball fan! As Ron Burgundy would say, "Stay classy, San Diego!"

Jack has also made a tradition out of wearing a birthday hat, complete with candles, when we go to games on his birthday; this definitely catches the eyes of some players, and they love being able to make a special day even more memorable by signing for a birthday boy! He has gotten some very prized autographs because of the hat. One is from Mark Melancon of the Pirates, who won the Trevor Hoffman award for relief pitching in 2015. Jack has also gotten some birthday autographs from Houston Street of the Angels and Sonny Gray of the A's, both very skilled All-Star pitchers.

Approaching players is a very different experience when they are not in and around the field. As is to be expected, politeness goes a long way towards getting a player in the mood to sign some autographs. A number of players are happy to sign autographs for kids. Kids tend to exude a natural excitement and wonder that truly makes them the best and most honest fans of the game. Adults looking for autographs are sometimes trying to gather up a bunch to sell, and their sometimes business-like attitude can be off-putting.

For both types of interactions, we found a little bit of research to be useful. If you are looking to get an autograph from a particular player, it helps to have something to say and present that sets you apart. As we discussed before, commenting on a certain play, or good result from a recent game, will earn you some smiles and good will, but another thing to take into consideration is the impact of what you're presenting to be autographed might have. Balls, bats, and cards are easily sold, and are established and common collector's items. Players are used to seeing them, and used to handling them. More personal items, on the other hand, like books, tend to pique players' interests. For example, our family book of photographs has become the boys' main way of collecting autographs, and it offers the perfect opener: "Hi, [insert name], would you like to sign our family book? Over the past five summers, we took the boys to all the stadiums, and we made this book as a memory. Would you sign this page at your stadium?" Several times, we have gotten a surprised, "Wow! I haven't even been to all the stadiums!" from an excited player.

Family traditions can double as great attention grabbers and give you an advantage when seeking autographs. Starting when Heath Bell was closer for the Padres, around 2010, there was a Yoda backpack that started traveling with the team from the bullpen to the dugout. We have run into Heath several times, and he is always incredibly friendly with kids. A true ambassador for the game. It was a rookie's job to carry it, and it was full of supplies for the players—sunflower seeds and things like that. Ashley Eckstein, wife of former infielder David Eckstein, is a huge Star Wars fan and voice actress for several Star Wars animated series, and her fandom rubbed off on the other players a bit. On a whim one day, we bought the boys a similar looking Yoda doll to bring to a game, in the off-chance that the players would like it. They did, and Yoda has ended up accompanying us to many Padres games. The players get a kick out of it, and really appreciate that their fans would come up with clever little ways to get their attention. The Yoda doll has gotten us many autographs and smiles, especially when he is wearing a wig and sunglasses!

The Yoda theme actually ended up going quite a bit farther than planned. We started taking Yoda to Padres games out of town, and after a few more weeks, other people started wearing Yoda-themed attire to Petco. Eventually, several members of the Padres marketing department asked us about our sons and what would they think of a Star Wars theme night. At one point, Grant actually went to Petco in a full Yoda costume, right in the middle of the promotional buzz around Star Wars, and was on TV with Jack. Kids were running up to him and asking for pictures! For a few games in September of that year, Yoda himself even announced the starting nine for the Padres over the loudspeaker, extolling Adrian Gonzalez in particular to "use the Force." Gonzalez was in his last year with the Padres, and had been something of a star for San Diego. He would end the season as team MVP for the third time in a row, so he must have taken Yoda's advice to heart! The Yoda doll has gotten the boys and their friends on the Jumbotron several times (and gotten some free popcorn every once in a while), which of course makes them enjoy going to the games even more than they already do. All in all, it was a fun time for the San Diego players and fans, and now several ballparks have Star Wars traditions and events. In fact, in the age of new Star Wars movies, the celebration is bigger and better than ever before. Announcers dress up as the villains, and portraits of Padres players souped up in Photoshop to look like the heroes glow brightly on the Jumbotron. Even the Friar has been seen wielding his own green lightsaber. We aren't sure if this theme started in San Diego, but that was first we ever saw of it, back in the summer of 2010! The boys have grown a bit now, and our beloved Yoda mascot has entered into retirement, but we always had a great time with him around. Now our Yoda relaxes above the dugout at the boys' rec games, keeping a close eye on the field!

We often incorporate costumes into our game day traditions. The wigs are always fun, and are another easy way to get a player's attention. When we were in Toronto for the Blue Jays game against the Royals, we were doing our thing before the game, watching the warm-up, cheering the players, and occasionally chatting with one or getting an autograph. The boys were wearing their brightly colored wigs, and José Mijares, pitcher at that time for the Royals, thought it was hilarious. He came over and asked to borrow one, and wore it for the rest of the warmup. Afterwards, he signed balls for the boys, gaining two fans for life. We were rooting for him after he was traded to the Giants, with whom he ended up winning the World Series in 2012.

This is the sort of thing that we really hope other families put a spin on. A fun toy, a sign, a certain costume scheme; there are many ways to set yourselves apart as fans in the hopes of getting autographs, bonding with the players, and meeting new friends. In this day and age, it is even easy to start a small following on Instagram or Facebook, and spread the fan fever that way!

So, after doing research on players, strategically placing yourself around warm ups, talking to players, and fighting the crowds for some well-earned and highly prized autographs, you have a bunch of signed balls, cards, bats, and more. What do you do with them? Most of the signed balls are kept in wire baskets on display. They are handled infrequently enough that we don't need to worry about the integrity of the signature, and are kept out of the way of any direct sunlight that might fade the ink. Some of the more personal balls, signed by favorite players or Hall of Famers, are kept behind glass. If you would like to individually store and protect your balls, there are many options. The high-quality, authentic MLB balls actually come in clear plastic boxes when purchased, which work great as a permanent storage and display solution. We recommend you label the outside of the plastic display case with the player's name. Jack has kept a few of these, and keeps them on his desk. Bats are beautiful items to display on walls. The boys take great pride in their collection, and have struck a good balance between preservation and display.

We also have a collection of baseball cards, some signed, and some rare. Most baseball card packs have runs of cards that are rarer and more valuable, with the rarity schema often detailed somewhere on the pack's foil wrapper. Keep an eye out for these! For the most part the cards are kept in three-ring binders organized by year, but the best signed and rare cards are kept in a special place in Dayna's desk. Signed cards can actually be tricky to store. Newer cards often have a glossy finish, which makes it difficult for them to retain the ink of a Sharpie. The ink has a hard time sticking to the gloss, and will start to separate and bubble after a few minutes, ruining the autograph. Thankfully, there is an easy fix, if you are planning on making premium signed cards a major part of your collection. Just give the part of the card that will be signed a quick once-over with an eraser to take off the very top layer of gloss finish, and you are good to go. Older cards are generally matte, and very easily take a nice, permanent signature, so no special preparations need to be made. The trading aspect of card collecting is very fun, and the boys love having friends over to look at the cards and make some trades.

We will note that taking cards to games can be cumbersome, and they are easy to bend, tear, or lose, as Grant can sadly attest to. If you do plan on bringing cards to be signed, consider affixing them to a piece of cardstock or Oxford spiral-bound index cards with adhesive photo corners. This will make the cards you need easy to get to, and you lower the risk of bending them.

Don't limit yourself to these common items for your personal collection, though. There are many options when it comes to commemorating your trips to stadiums, your full tour of all the MLB ballparks, or a special connection you feel to certain fields in particular. Think of something unique to your family that you would like to have signed by players along the way. We have several signed books, for example, and interesting stories to go along with them.

We were lucky to meet Tony Gwynn, right fielder for the Padres and one of the best hitters in MLB history, in 2007. We were at the Chicago O'Hare International Airport, and ran into him before our flight. He was returning to San Diego from his Hall of Fame induction. Grant was four at the time, but he had been introduced to Tony via his baseball card; Steve had always told Grant that this was a very special card. So when

Steve asked Grant in the terminal who was on the card that he should always respect, Grant replied confidently, "Tony Gwynn!" Tony smiled and gave him a high-five, then signed a book Steve had about him. Later on, at the San Diego airport, we saw him again at the baggage claim! Grant started waving across the conveyor belt and yelling, "Hi, Tony Gwynn!" at the top of his lungs. You could, at that moment, hear a pin drop in the San Diego airport! We looked up and sure enough, there was Tony, waiting for his bags. He was very gracious again, and looked over at Grant, smiled, and gave him a wave back. It was a very special moment for us. Tony passed away in 2014 after a storied career in which he played for the Padres for twenty years, and he will be missed. It's never too early to teach your kids about the game and the players, and get them excited about them. Had we waited to introduce Grant to Tony's card and its significance to Padres' fans until he was older, he never would have gotten as much out of the experience of meeting him. Here is another tip this experience taught us; while you should be careful not to over-pack, including a few mementos in your luggage as you travel the country for ballgames can pay off in unexpected ways.

It is common, when a new stadium is built, for souvenirs from the previous stadium to be made available for purchase. There are a handful of seats from the old Yankee stadium for sale online, for example, and you can find everything from posters to signs to bricks from stadiums of years past. In fact, the secondary market for souvenirs from demolished stadiums is large enough, and the collectors' appetites fierce enough, that when word went out that the Met's last game at Shea Stadium would be in early October of 2008, park management had to hire additional security to keep fans from sneaking off with pieces of the stadium! Even dirt and grass from the field itself was eyed by a few overeager fans.

One of the things we did to memorialize our love of baseball and commemorate the importance it has for our family was to purchase a brick from the partial deconstruction of the previous Padres' park, Qualcomm Stadium, inscribe it with the family name, and have it installed at the Tony Gwynn statue at Petco. We actually missed our initial opportunity to get these bricks when they were first for sale, but there was a secondary sale in May of 2007 and we were ready. When an extension was being put up at Petco, the Padres sold memorial bricks there as well, for a reasonable price. After we purchased one of these bricks, the team sent us a replica copy. Steve keeps ours displayed in his man cave inspired by the Dan Patrick show, a constant reminder of our contribution to the growth of our Padres. Our brick at the Tony Gwynn statue proudly proclaims, "Let's Go Padres!" and includes the date of Gwynn's induction into the Hall of Fame. It is wonderful for our family to have this permanent part of Padres and baseball history, under the watchful eye of a San Diego icon and legendary baseball star that we got to meet. This is a unique way to tie your family to the ballpark, and it is something we hope our children will look back on fondly in the future.

CHAPTER FIVE
Brands Matter

Loyalty, a great attitude, and engaging with those you meet can be very rewarding! We really had a blast when we visited our nation's capital to watch the Washington Nationals play in 2012. Dayna's father, brother, and sister (Pap Pap, Uncle Dean, and Aunt Doe) joined us. We visited downtown D.C., and saw the White House, the National Monument, and Ford's Theatre (where President Lincoln was assassinated). We also visited the International Spy Museum, and had an amazing time even before we headed down to the game.

Professional baseball in Washington, D.C. has an interesting history. The city was home to one of the original eight teams in the American League, known then as the Washington Senators. They were chartered in 1901, and in 1905 became the Nationals. Their uniforms were modified in 1907 to remove the "Nationals" moniker, and for the next fifty years they were alternately known as the Senators, the Nationals, or simply "W", after the letter that emblazoned their uniforms. They played for several years at a wooden stadium known as Nationals Park that burned down in 1911, and then the more modern stadium that replaced it at the same location in the city some months later. For many years they were owned and managed by Clark Griffith, after whom this new stadium was renamed in 1920. The Griffith family managed the Nationals until Clark's son Calvin eventually brokered a deal to relocate the team to Minnesota in 1960, where they became the Twins. Another team, also named the Senators, was born, and played out of RFK, one of the first multipurpose stadiums in the nation, until they moved to Arlington and became the Texas Rangers in 1972. RFK lived on, primarily as a football and now soccer stadium, but there was no major league baseball team in the city for decades.

In 1969, the first Canadian major league team, the Montreal Expos, was formed. The Expos enjoyed a thirty-five-year tenure in the major leagues until 2001, when the MLB voted to contract the league by two teams—the Expos and the Twins. This was a very contentious decision, and after many twists and turns, it was repealed in the courts after the teams had already been somewhat disbanded. Suddenly, the Expos were without hometown ownership, and found themselves splitting the 2003 and 2004 seasons between some overseas stadiums and Montreal. Washington courted the team, and eventually the Expos moved to D.C., where they became the Nationals.

As part of the agreement to bring the team to the city, D.C. needed to build a new stadium, quickly. While the newly minted Nationals made do at RFK, D.C. seized twenty-one acres of real estate in the Southeast quadrant through eminent domain and started building in 2006. In order to build a new stadium from the ground up in less than two years, the design and construction were done in concert, on the ground. It opened in 2008, and there were still signs of construction around the stadium when we attended, four years later. There wasn't much to do right around the stadium, but it sits right next to the Navy Yard Metro, so all of D.C. is yours to explore before and after the games.

Walking up to Nationals Park that day, we were surprised by how different the atmosphere was from Camden Yards in Baltimore, just forty miles away. We had attended an Orioles game at Camden Yards a week before, and we had loved the warmth of the brick stadium. Built on the site of Babe Ruth's childhood home, it is very retro and classic-looking, but with all the modern amenities. When the Orioles were designing their stadium, they were working in a more established part of their city, for a highly celebrated and entrenched team. It was built with the intention of providing the ultimate fan experience, and influenced an entire new generation of baseball stadiums. The designers captured a lot of the traditional baseball feeling, eschewing the cookie-cutter styles that dominated a lot of stadiums in the 1980s. Building against the old B&O Warehouse, Camden has a beautiful view of the downtown Baltimore skyline and is close to the Inner Harbor. It has a really cool downtown city feel, not like you're leaving the main part of the city for another destination. It has a traditional concourse, behind the stands, which means you can't wander around and still watch the field.

Nationals Park is much more modern looking, designed with glass and cast concrete to mimic the limestone of other iconic buildings around the city. The small road that leads from the Metro to the stadium is lined with shipping container bars and food trucks, offering fans the opportunity to pre-game in a neighborhood that hasn't built up a lot of other amenities yet. With a view of the Anacostia River and a grove of cherry trees, the main entrance opens up into centerfield. When you walk in, the stadium unfolds before you, and you get a taste for how airy and open the entire experience will be. The entrance has a big plaza where people can meet up, the Strike Zone (a kids' play area featuring a variety of games), and shows a great view of the Nationals' 4,811 square foot scoreboard. The stadium has very wide open concourses, and the designers organized the park in such a way that ensures guests can watch the game from almost anywhere on the grounds. The seating bowl is in three levels, but the open-air concourse allows you to see the game when you're walking around, getting food, etc. They thought of nearly every detail, even installing chest-high tables near the food stands so fans had a place to eat while watching the game. The Ring of Honor, celebrating players from the Washington Senators (Joe Cronin, Rick Ferrell, Goose Goslin, Clark Griffith, Bucky Harris, Walter Johnson, Harmon Killebrew, Heinie Manush, Sam Rice, and Early Wynn), the Homestead Grays (Cool Papa Bell, Ray Brown, Josh Gibson, Buck Leonard, Cumberland Posey, and Jud Wilson), and the Montreal Expos (Gary Carter and Andre Dawson) who have been inducted into the Baseball Hall of Fame, celebrates the players with interesting in-motion statues.

The day was hot and muggy, typical for summer in the District, but the crowd was abuzz. It was actually one of the hottest Julys on record for the area, and by the time it was getting dark out it was still well over ninety degrees. As we walked in and saw the scoreboard, we noticed it had been redesigned to look like a classic wooden scoreboard; throughout the evening, it also played video tributes to the 1924 Senators. The Nationals were celebrating a Turn Back the Clock night, in remembrance of the 1924 season, during which the Nationals had defeated the New York Giants in the World Series in a best of seven match (in a game historians rate as one of the best in the professional baseball annals). The Giants had moved in 1957 to San Francisco, and it was as the San Francisco Giants that they were facing the Nats that night. So, after over one hundred years of games, cross-country team relocations, and management politics, our family finally sat down with thousands of other fans to watch this symbolic reunion of two of the oldest ball clubs in the country. Pennants sporting the "W" logo and the year fluttered in the wind as the players took the field, both teams sporting replica 1924 jerseys. The Nationals were decked out in white with the classic "W" logo, while the Giants wore their vintage-looking pinstripe hats, upon which you could spot the New York logo (which was later adopted by the Mets at their inception in 1962). The players weren't the only ones dressed according to the time period; the grounds crew and other staff were dressed up as well in full 1920s attire, complete with skimmer hats and newsie caps. There was also traditional baseball organ music! This was the perfect game to attend on a road trip with Pap Pap. He was born in 1930, and the baseball he knew as a kid wasn't that far off from what the Nats were honoring that night.

Like most things baseball, music at games has its own history and evolution. The first time games were serenaded by live organ music was in 1941, when the practice was introduced at Wrigley field. Over time other stadiums adopted the practice, which in turn gave way to other trends, like individual theme songs for players and signature songs in the seventh-inning stretch. Live organ playing has been slowly reintroduced to the major leagues, and Nationals Park has been graced with the playing of organist Dr. Van Hoose since 2010. His playing gave the throwback event an authentic touch! Traditional organ music was played between innings, and the players used an organ rendition of their walk-up music. A 1920s-themed jazz orchestra played a performance before the game as well. Most of the noise, though, came from the fans, who got very into the game, despite the lack of loud recorded cues and the flashing scoreboards of most games. They clapped in rhythm and cheered loudly. The energy was very electric!

The most amazing thing about the preparations was that the opening pitch was performed with an actual ball from Game Six of the World Series in 1924. In keeping with the eye for historical detail the organizers had already displayed, the opening pitch was thrown from behind the home team dugout by Hank Thomas, grandson of the Nationals pitcher who had thrown for that winning 1924 team, Walter Johnson (who some consider to be the best pitcher ever). The modern ceremonial first pitch is from the pitcher's mound, but that night we were doing things in the old-school style! For many years the ball was thrown by the guest of honor from his or her seat in the stands, usually very close to the action. The way things are done now, with the guest actually throwing the pitch from the pitcher's mound, was first done by President Reagan in 1984 when he threw out the first pitch of Opening Day in Baltimore. It was cool to see this old method used, and using such a rare and unique ball was icing on the cake. The amount of care that goes into keeping such an old ball in such good condition must be immense, and we thought the opening throw was a great touch.

The Racing Presidents and Screech, some of the mascots associated with Nationals Park, also wore 1924 Senators jerseys. There was a race in the middle of the fourth inning (like the one between Pierogies in Pittsburgh and the Sausages in Milwaukee) between the Presidents (large headed Thomas Jefferson, Abraham Lincoln, Teddy Roosevelt, William Taft, and George Washington). When we attended, the "Let Teddy Win!" campaign was in full effect, and audience members even had shirts with the slogan on it. Teddy Roosevelt, in a running gag, had never won the Presidents Race, and his antics had gotten increasingly desperate and hilarious—he had been disqualified for riding a golf cart through the race, enlisted the help of visiting mascots to trip up the other Presidents, and held a longstanding grudge against the Oriole Bird for doing the same to him. He was finally allowed to win on the last regular season game that year. The event was clearly a fan favorite, and the kids got a kick out of it. The mascots were very interactive, and they were available before and after the game for photos.

The rest of the game was peppered with other throwbacks to the old baseball days, and it was definitely a treat for the fans. The first few thousand spectators who entered the stadium received replicas of the original 1924 World Series scorecard. Consistently voted as having some of the best food in baseball, the Nationals Park offered specials on concessions, with some popcorn, peanuts, and hot dogs available for a nickel around the park. Both teams stood together on the field during the National Anthem. There were some anachronisms, of course—unlike the 1924 games, the jerseys had numbers on the back (but no names), it was a night game, and they didn't throw out the modern batting helmets or catcher's gear! It was a great time and an interesting historical lesson.

The throwback game had been part of a series, and the Nationals had already won the first game the previous day by a whopping margin of 9 to 4. They were actually behind by two runs going into the ninth inning, though, and the home fans were restless. We were all decked out in our Nationals gear (modern gear, not replicas!) and were, as usual, cheering our hearts out for the home team. The Nats were able to tie the game at five runs apiece after a nice single from rookie of the year and future MVP, Bryce Harper. The end of the game was a tricky one. Harper had made it to third, and Zimmerman was on first, with one out on the books. The Nationals first baseman, Adam LaRoche, then hit a nonthreatening grounder that should very easily have been picked up for a double play, sending the game to extra innings as a tie. As it happened, though, after getting the first out on second, the Giants infielder messed up the throw to first. It skipped past the Giants first baseman. Harper had been running from the moment he heard the crack of the bat, and scored the game winning run. It wasn't the prettiest of game-winning plays, but we were still happy! It was also very historically appropriate, because the Senators had won on a walk-off during that 1924 game as well!

A Haferkamp game wouldn't be complete without a getting a few autographs, and this game was no exception. During the latter half of the game, we journeyed to the outfield walls to see if we could chat with some players and offer encouragement. During the seventh inning, Harper himself tossed the boys a ball! It's not every day you get a ball from a rookie of the year who would in two short innings score the winning run. Bryce pretended not to see them after they rushed up, excited that he was so close, and he acted as though he was going to throw the ball back out to the field. Suddenly he spun around and threw it right to them. The boys may not have seen his good-natured deception, but Uncle Dean certainly did! Jack and Grant also got an autograph from noble bald eagle Screech, the Nationals mascot. All that practice getting autographs from Disney characters really paid off here!

This game was also historically important to our family—it was the halfway point of our first extensive baseball stadium tour trip. In prior years, we had mostly gone to games and stadiums when they were convenient—near our home, one-off trips, or near family we were visiting. This was our first full tour, and we hit six stadiums and saw six games over the course of eleven days. We had started with the Orioles at Camden Yards, then gone up to see the Blue Jays in Toronto, then down to a Pirates game in Pittsburgh, on to the Nats game in DC, then the Phillies in Citizens Bank Park, and ended with a Mets game in Citi Field. We were already heading to Pennsylvania for a family wedding, and we knew the kids were getting older and were better prepared for a more extensive trip. It ended up being our longest trip of the entire journey, and we covered the most stadiums in one go. We took two big trips the next year in 2013, and finished off with another big trip in 2014. These multi-stadium trips put our skills to the test, and taught us all more about the planning and budgeting process. We learned a lot of great techniques, and made connections with brands that helped us plan for places we weren't as familiar with when we were on a tight schedule.

———————— ◆ ————————

Before we had even started on our quest to visit all thirty stadiums as a family, we had already attended many games together at Petco and PNC. By the time we started our 2012 trip, we had already visited Angel Stadium of Anaheim and Chase Field in 2009, Coors Field and Progressive Field in 2010, and Fenway Park, Sun Life Stadium, Tropicana Field, and Yankee Stadium in 2011. We had ten stadiums under our belts already, with twenty left to go.

Steve is an extreme planner, who enjoys plotting and mapping everything out the old-fashioned way. Pulling out a pencil and paper and looking up the schedules for the various teams on the Internet, he sat down and calculated the possibilities. For our 2012 trip, we knew we had as home base the wedding we were attending in Pennsylvania. Steve charted out a path that would ultimately take us several thousand miles, through Niagara Falls and back, ultimately finishing off in New York at Citi Field. It took a lot of finagling to make it all work, and a lot of quality time together in the car! We were able to hit up a game at AT&T Park in San Francisco later that summer, and by the end of 2012, we had been to sixteen stadiums—over half!

This method worked well, and it became our go-to approach towards planning. Every time we knew we were traveling somewhere or really wanted to see a certain game, Steve would pull out our maps and lists and the schedules and get to work. Before the beginning of each season, we'd ask the kids which stadiums they thought they wanted to go to next, and try to figure that into our plans. He would guarantee a certain area of the US, and start scribbling notes on interstates, flight times, and hotel rates.

It was important to us that we fit these trips into our busy lives, and not make the journey all-consuming. We had certainly heard stories, and met people who were trying to hit all the stadiums in one summer, or even in one month, but that was never our goal. We were conscious of keeping these trips fun and growing together as a family, not creating a situation where it became overly taxing or stressful.

Baseball is a big part of our lives outside of going to ballgames. Steve had been helping coach the boys' team through LCYO for years, as well as the local Little League, and we have been ingrained in the community ever since, and have followed the seasons all the way through to our own Pony League youth baseball All-Star team. Dayna operated the team Shutterfly site and photography, and helped with finding sponsors. Steve was coaching before the trip started, and continued all the way through the end. Once or twice that got us into a little bit of a situation, when the Pony League schedule ran up against our stadium tour agenda. Once or twice our trips would be carefully planned out for the summer, and then the kids would make the All-Star team and have games scheduled for the same days we would be gone. There were two summers that we just had to apologize and let everyone know that we would be out of town for some of the games. We were committed to going on this journey while the kids were young. It was a little bit of a sacrifice; throughout the whole thing, we missed practices and games over spring breaks as well, and we had to try and work all of our trips within certain time parameters. It's not like we had a whole summer to be on the road, so we basically did it when we were already traveling. We never spent more than ten or eleven days away. At this point, we can look back and say we're glad we did our trips and participated in the boys' All-Stars—striking that type of balance gave us the best of both worlds.

Having now completed the entire stadium tour, we have learned quite a few lessons. When we take these trips in the future, we're going to be more careful to give ourselves more time to explore the cities and enjoy the stadiums and games. We wish, for example, that we would have had more time in Baltimore at Camden Yards. Next time, we're going to take a few more days for stops close to stadiums. We keep bucket lists for future trips that include Lambeau Field in Milwaukee and the Baseball Hall of Fame in Cooperstown. Before beginning the trip, we wish we would have known to go early and stay the whole game, and never rush the time at the stadiums. This was something we ended up doing later on in the tour. We advise planning on taking in two games per stadium, with a little room in the schedule in case of a rainout or a cancelled game. We lucked out—we had a few games called after six innings, but we had another game planned for the next day as backup. It would have been a drag to have been at one of the more difficult to access stadiums, like Safeco in Seattle, and not have been able to see a game!

One of the nicest parts about not rushing the stadium tour journey is that it gives you more flexibility when it comes to what part of the season you're going to visit each location during. The MLB stadiums range across the entire U.S., plus Toronto, which means there are more and less ideal times to visit based on the weather. Toronto in April is still very cold, and is a very different experience from a game in Phoenix in August—and neither are ideal. Some stadiums in extreme climates, like Safeco in Seattle, Washington, and Tropicana Field in St. Petersburg, Florida, are enclosed or partially enclosed, so you won't necessarily experience a lot of rain-outs, but getting to and from the stadium, as well as enjoying the city and surrounding sites, will be more enjoyable in certain months. In case you have the luxury of planning your trip around the best time of the baseball season to visit each of these places, here's what we recommend:

Stadium (Team)	Location	Best Month	Weather Stats
Angel Stadium of Anaheim (Angels)	Anaheim, CA	May	High-80 Low-60
AT&T Park (Giants)	San Francisco, CA	September	High-70 Low-55 Warmest time of year, still dry
Busch Stadium (Cardinals)	St. Louis, MO	May	High-76 Low-57 Lowest humidity

Chase Field (Diamondbacks)	Phoenix, AZ	April	High-85
			Low-60
			Cool for AZ, dry, sunny
Citi Field (Mets)	Queens, NY	June	High-79
			Low-63
			Warm, not too humid yet
Citizens Bank Park (Phillies)	Philadelphia, PA	June	High-82
			Low-64
			Warm, sunny, not too humid yet
Comerica Park (Tigers)	Detroit, MI	June	High-79
			Low-59
			Warm, sunny, not too humid yet
Coors Field (Rockies)	Denver, CO	September	High-78
			Low-48
			Best temperatures and most sunny days
Dodger Stadium (Dodgers)	Los Angeles, CA	May	High-74
			Low-57
			Not too hot yet and after rainy season
Fenway Park (Red Sox)	Boston, MA	July	High-81
			Low-65
			Warm and sunny
Globe Life Park (Rangers)	Arlington, TX	April	High-73
			Low-54
			Cool for TX, low rainfall
Great American Ball Park (Reds)	Cincinnati, OH	May	High-73
			Low-53
			Warm, not too humid yet
Kauffman Stadium (Royals)	Kansas City, MO	May	High-74
			Low-54
			Warm, not too humid yet

Marlins Park (Marlins)	Miami, FL	April	High-83
			Low-68
			Before rainy season, not too hot
Miller Park (Brewers)	Milwaukee, WI	July	High-80
			Low-63
			Most sunshine
Minute Maid Park (Astros)	Houston, TX	April	High-79
			Low-59
			Best temperature/ rainfall mix
Nationals Park (Nationals)	Washington, DC	May	High-75
			Low-56
			Warm, sunny, not too humid yet
O.co Coliseum (Athletics)	Oakland, CA	August	High-73
			Low-57
			Warm and dry
Oriole Park at Camden Yards (Orioles)	Baltimore, MD	May	High-75
			Low-56
			Warm, sunny, not too humid yet
Petco Park (Padres)	San Diego, CA	September	High-75
			Low-65
			Best temperature/ sunshine mix
PNC Park (Pirates)	Pittsburgh, PA	June	High-79
			Low-58
			Warm, sunny, not too humid
Progressive Field (Indians)	Cleveland, OH	June	High-78
			Low-60
			Warm and sunny
Rogers Centre (Indians)	Toronto, ON, CA	July	High-79
			Low-64
			Warm and sunny

Safeco Field (Mariners)	Seattle, WA	July	High-75
			Low-55
			Warm, sunny, low humidity
Target Field (Twins)	Minneapolis, MN	June	High-78
			Low-58
			Warm, sunny, low humidity
Tropicana Field (Rays)	St. Petersburg, FL	April	High-81
			Low-64
			Warm and dry
Turner Field (Braves)	Atlanta, GA	May	High-79
			Low-60
			Best temperature/ sunshine/ humidity mix
U.S. Cellular Field (White Sox)	Chicago, IL	June	High-79
			Low-58
			Warm, sunny, not too humid
Wrigley Field (Cubs)	Chicago, IL	June	High-79
			Low-58
			Warm, sunny, not too humid
Yankee Stadium	Bronx, NY	June	High-79
			Low-63
			Warm, not too humid yet

When you're looking at the schedules and choosing games, pay attention to theme nights and special events at the stadiums! Each stadium offers several giveaways and promos each season, and we have caught many games on those days. It's a great way to experience new things at the games, get into a different vibe, and collect interesting souvenirs.

There are promo nights, when the teams will do giveaways of bobbleheads, t-shirts and jerseys, sweatshirts, hats, blankets, bags, mugs and cups—all sorts of gear! Some of these promos feature items that aren't available in the gift shops, making them even more intriguing to the serious souvenir hunters in our family. The crowds get really competitive, since there are usually a limited number (most promo nights we've seen have been capped somewhere around the first 10,000 guests, and sometimes there are age restrictions as well), but you can meet great people and have wonderful conversations in the lines with others who are as interested in baseball and excited as you are! I think the second-longest line we've ever stood in was for the Hank Aaron bobblehead at a Brewers game at Miller Park in Milwaukee. We've gotten a "Let's Go Bucs!" pillow from PNC, a Vin Scully bobblehead from Dodger Stadium, a Pirates helmet from PNC, and a Josh Donaldson bobblehead from Oakland Coliseum, among many other promo giveaways. They're special reminders for us of those games, and we display them proudly with our other souvenirs and mementos from the trips.

Each stadium also usually hosts some special event games through the year, highlighting spring and summer holidays like Independence Day, Mother's and Father's Day, and special team anniversary days. We first visited the Angel Stadium as a family on Mother's Day 2009, and it was a wonderful way to spend a special day all together. They gave out pink Angels' bags to all the mothers, and Dayna had a great time with the boys, doing something we all love!

Angel Stadium is a solid, old-school ball park. It has hosted several MLB All-Star games (including the first to ever be televised), as well as professional football games. It is an easy choice when it comes to baseball-loving families choosing a vacation spot, as the stadium is just a few miles away from Disneyland in Anaheim, California! The Angels themselves are one of the teams that sprouted up during the expansion era of the 1960s, and have undergone a handful of name changes as well. The Rally Monkey that our family loves so much originated with the Angels, and we definitely enjoy having the chance to make it out to Anaheim to catch a game!

Theme nights are always exciting! They're also a great way to get people who might not be as into baseball more pumped for the games. In addition to the ones we have mentioned so far, we've been to theme nights for cancer and autism awareness, where a portion of the proceeds goes to charitable institutions associated with the cause. There are career-specific theme nights, for members of the armed services and law enforcement, among others—the Marine Salute at Petco Park on Sundays is always very special to see. We saw a great game with an energized crowd during University of Miami Night at Marlins Park. There are purely fun theme days—retro, dance parties, zombie days, Ghostbusters, Game of Thrones, superheroes, movies on the field, bat days, trivia nights, and doggie days (when you can bring your pup to watch the game with you!).

Obviously it's unlikely you'll be able to go to exclusively special and themed nights during trips where you're hitting up several stadiums, but we highly recommend taking a look through the options and hitting up the ones that interest you and your family for individual games and stadium trips.

Carefully tracking flights and travel between stadiums isn't easy, but it isn't overly difficult either. We carefully planned out our travels between the stadiums to reach our goals, make the games, and minimize our time in the car. When booking flights to farther locations, we would try and get in as early as possible in case we needed to fly on game days. Even with the best planning, we still had one or two flights that got into a city at four o'clock, and the game would be at seven, and it always made us a little nervous—what if the flight was delayed? We got lucky and never missed a game due to flight delays, but we still always provided ourselves an extra day buffer for that type of travel. An extra day and another game in a harder-to-reach city allowed us to relax and worry less about potential rain outs and flight delays and really enjoy our trips.

Some of our big stadium tours might look circuitous, but it was all on purpose. We tried to set a four-to-six-hour limit on drive times, so that travel between games never felt like a chore. Luckily, for most of these trips, travel time was closer to two hours from city to city. We would hop from stadium to stadium, not feeling drained from a long car ride, and then loop out and find a game we could go to as our last destination before flying home. We were able to avoid most backtracking, and keep the rides calm while hitting the maximum number of stadiums in a given large geographical area.

We definitely tried not only to minimize the pain of traveling, but to actually build in the fun and excitement! When it comes down to it, most baseball games are going to be four hours or less; as a result, much of our time was spent on the journey itself, spending time together and exploring new things. We started this practice early, as you might recall, when we hired a school bus to take twenty-two members of our extended family to a PNC Pirates game, and it was a blast! We highly recommend making the travel to games part of the entertainment—we see people with RVs and stretch limos tailgating and having a great time at the stadiums with big parking lots (like the Brewers!). Shuttles from the hotels near the stadium to the games are usually a party, and it's great to see everyone so excited and in team colors. The kids also love taking public transportation around cities that have it—we don't have underground subways near us in San Diego, so it's always an adventure to them in other big cities! Riding the Amtrak train from Grand Central Station while visiting Yankee Stadium in New York to Fenway in Boston was awesome, definitely a highlight of the journey. It was the boys' first time on a train, and they were thrilled! We also rented tandem bikes to explore Boston when we arrived, and have taken many tour buses around cities—using less commonplace transportation makes every trip a cool learning experience.

Before you even head out the door, make sure you know and have exactly the right paperwork for your trip! We spent a tough day in Seattle, trying to get onto our flight to Vancouver, because we didn't realize the kids would need passports to board. When we had driven into Toronto, birth certificates had been fine, and we were very surprised the same requirements weren't honored at the airport. We adjusted, rented a car, drove up, and had a great time, but it was a frustrating experience trying to board our flight, and we lucked out that Vancouver is really only a three hour drive from Seattle—imagine if we had been trying to get to Calgary! It was a good lesson for us to learn, and we double check now that all our traveling papers, tickets, maps, and other useful paperwork are organized in a binder before we hit the road.

While we often try to find Marriott hotels near the stadiums in order to take advantage of our customer loyalty points, we also pay close attention to other hotels within walking distance to the stadium or that offer shuttles. Marriott hotels, and some other chains like Hyatt, are a favorite with professional athletes, because they are so ubiquitous and work very hard to earn player loyalty. This is a great reason to consider supporting Marriott for your hotel stay—there's a chance you'll be staying in the same hotel as members of the traveling team! There are many different hotels near almost every MLB stadium that offer special packages for baseball fans, and they sometimes include complimentary tickets. They can be a great value for people traveling from out of town, especially couples. They can sometimes even be found through hotel discount websites, which have their own loyalty programs and will give you additional rewards. Some stadiums, like Rogers Centre in Toronto, have hotels that overlook the stadium itself from rooftop pools or even rooms, and can be a cool, unique way to experience a live game! Shop around and see what the area has to offer.

Prepping for each stadium beforehand and knowing the layout and amenities can really make your visits go more smoothly and give you time to kick back and just enjoy the trip. Consider your family's needs, and do a little research beforehand to make sure you're going to have the best experience. Since we're very into autographs, we were glad to know beforehand that the Oakland Coliseum allows you to take in bats for autographs, unlike the majority of stadiums.

We've been very glad that we knew exactly where to find the lost and found at multiple stadiums. With the excitement of the game and the plethora of mementos we collect, we've lost a handful of mementos. At AT&T Park Jack lost a glove, and the lost and found folks were instrumental in helping us get it back. Always put your number on a glove! It doesn't always pan out (we never were able to recover Grant's cards from the Great American Ballpark) but it is definitely information worth having!

There is a customer service desk at all stadiums, and often they give first game certificates or other neat stuff, such as stickers, to kids. Guest services also usually has a pocket guide for the dining options in the park, which is very useful. They can tell you a lot about the stadium and the teams and their histories, which can both be very educational and save you a lot of time. Customer service people seem to really love their jobs, and will be happy to share cool stories about their wild experiences at the stadium!

It's not a bad plan to have a survival kit for being at the stadium, especially if someone in your group has special needs or is a young child. Many stadiums have size limits on bags, but a small drawstring nylon bag of essentials will help you out. Double check with the stadium you're heading to beforehand to make sure you can bring everything in (the rules fluctuate from stadium to stadium), but we like to suggest you pack a travel poncho and sunscreen for open air stadiums, all of the materials you'll need for autographs, unopened water bottles and snacks for smaller children, and whatever personalized items you'll need. Having all of these things together in an easy to grab go-bag will save you a lot of hassle digging around your car and baggage at the last moment.

Baseball has always been a great activity for us to do together because the stadiums are pretty safe and family friendly, and the crowds are very polite in comparison with some other major league sports. Still, it never hurts to take a few safety precautions before you go into a game, especially if you have children. If you're with infants or people with mobility issues, it's better to find seats in which there's no threat of being hit with a foul ball or broken bat. Although most baseball crowds are great, there are still some bitter rivalries, and things can get heated; if you're concerned about that, check out the special family nights available at most stadiums. There are ID bracelets available at every customer service counter, in case you get separated from your child.

In fact, we had a terrifying moment at the Park at the Park in Petco many years ago when Jack was two years old. He suddenly wandered off and went missing for nearly twenty minutes. It was utter chaos before we found him in a play tunnel at the playground area. You often think things won't happen to you, but in an instant they can! In addition to getting ID bracelets, common sense and basic preparation will go a long way towards preventing this kind of thing—be aware of your surroundings, teach your children your phone number (and place the number on temporary safety tattoos!) and family rules about what to do if they are lost, and have a plan with your group for where you'll meet if something comes up.

Finally, when you're scheduling and planning, don't forget about the special event perks that many stadiums offer. Ballparks have special tours and activities that you can take part in, as long as you schedule ahead. We've taken tours at Petco, Chase Field, Coors, Fenway, Great American Ballpark, Busch, and Wrigley, and we've learned so much from each one! While you're planning, consider whether you'd like to send a message to your group on the Jumbotron (we've sent messages for birthdays before, and it's a great way to show your love). If you're planning a REALLY special occasion...all but five of the MLB stadiums offer unique ways of asking that special someone for their hand in marriage, some of which are really funny and cool! We've seen several marriage proposals, and we love the ones that the mascots get involved in. When you go to a game you can call ahead of time, and if you have a large enough group you can ask that the mascot come by your section at some point in the game. We have done this a few times at PNC Park when we had big family groups.

———◆—————

We are glad we didn't sit down and figure out the entire total cost prior to starting the journey—it would have been very daunting. Since we split the trips over several years, we were able to crunch the numbers and incorporate the costs into expenses we would have undertaken anyways. There's no way we would have missed certain family events on the East Coast, and we were able to springboard off those tickets to spend time at far-away baseball stadiums. Dayna's work travels took her to many cities, and on occasion we were able to go with her and spend time at games and explore the towns while she took care of business. As a family, we carefully considered and budgeted for our most valued experiences year by year.

Everyone's budget and finances will look different, as they start to consider their own journeys, but one of the most valuable tips we picked up along the way was to get tickets whenever possible for back-to-back nights at each stadium. We would generally get good seats (which usually came with higher price tags) the first night, so that we could enjoy the game, and then we would pick up cheaper tickets the next day so we could spend more time walking around, exploring the stadium, and taking part in other activities. Every stadium offers highly discounted tickets for certain games and certain seats—sometimes as low as five to ten dollars! These might not be for the most anticipated games or the best seats in the house, but modern baseball stadiums have so much more to offer than just the game. Cheaper tickets allow for you to have fun with the kids' areas and games, look at the statues and art, explore the architecture and landscaping, take your time in the gift shop, and sample the varieties of foods offered. Splitting the experience between the better seats one night and the stadium tours the next really was a great compromise that again gave us the best of both worlds.

We always included a significant cushion in our budgets for souvenirs. When people walk into our home, Steve often hears the joke, "Your wife must love baseball!" Going to games as a family is one of our favorite activities, and our home reflects all of our awesome memories. We have collected mementos from every stadium we have visited. Jack usually got a team hat, Grant focused on team shirts with players' names on the back.

Our funniest gift store moment was in Arlington, Texas, on opening day for the Rangers. The gift shop, as you can imagine, was packed, an absolute zoo. Dayna was in there trying to get souvenirs for the kids, and after waiting in line for a bit, finally got to the counter. They rang her up and said, "Okay, it's your lucky day, and you get an oversized canvas ticket for your wall!" We hadn't even known the promotion was going on! The kids were very excited. It really felt like we had won the lottery. The ticket ended up being one of our more memorable gift store keepsakes, and it's still hanging on the wall. We are cost conscious, and so when we came to the point where we realized we'd be buying something everywhere to commemorate our visits, we definitely decided to be a little more frugal and work it into our budget.

One time, we had allowed Jack to pick out one souvenir. We were in downtown New York City, so you can imagine the prices! He found a fitted ball cap, which we had embroidered with his name on the back. It was a very cool hat, one of a kind now that his name was on it, and it cost $55.00. It was doubly special since it was his birthday! Well, we had gotten it right before we hopped on the train to Boston. We had arrived and disembarked when Jack realized he had already lost the hat. The train had already left, but Steve wasn't going to stand to lose such a wonderful and pricey souvenir and immediately jumped into superhero mode. We'd had the hat for less than twenty-four hours, and there was no way he was just going to let that money be flushed away! He figured out where the train was headed, and jumped on another train to catch up with it. Dayna and the kids were convinced he would never find it, and so were the conductors when he asked to be let back on the train. He looked under all the seats and finally found the hat. He arrived back at the hotel, a little frustrated that the journey had taken two hours, but ultimately victorious. It made us more mindful of keeping track of our mementos and souvenirs!

Some of our favorite souvenirs have been much less expensive, or even free. One of the absolute best mementos we have is the digital scrapbook that Dayna made for the boys on Shutterfly, which captured some of our favorite memories and is always accessible online. It took her three months to make it perfect, and we love it! We ordered hard copies for the boys for Christmas as a special gift, and it's become a great place to get additional autographs as well.

We were having an in-ground pool installed, and the workers had gotten to the point where the space was all dug out and the concrete was ready to be poured for its foundation. Before doing that, we told them to hold on a minute, and Jack ran to get a ball. We each signed it: Daddyo,

Mommo, Grant, and Jack, and then we scribbled on our favorite teams too. Finally, we finished off with "Let's Hit 'Em All!" right on the sweet spot, and tossed it in. The concrete was poured, the pool was built, and we now have a permanent, hidden reminder of this great journey we made together as a family.

Prior to beginning the journey, we wish we would have known about the MLB Passport book. It's a reasonably priced leather booklet that you can get stamped at each stadium, and it has stickers and maps for the seats you had, and folders to hold ticket stubs. Ideas like this are fantastic for anyone who doesn't have a big budget to spend on souvenirs, or needs a more compact way to store their memorabilia. We recommend keeping your ticket stubs in a frame or in a book, and scrapbooking stadium hand-outs and family photos is another inexpensive, portable option.

It's important to explore deals through brands, credit cards, and loyalty points programs. Dayna's career with Federated has always in-volved traveling across the U.S., so fortunately for us, she's accumulated a lot of customer loyalty points over the years that we were able to use to defray some of our costs. She prefers traveling on Southwest, staying at Marriott hotels, and renting from National, and since all are so ubiq-uitous in the U.S., we were able to cash in on those loyalty points for many of our trips, effectively flying and lodging for free in some places. It definitely helped soften the financial blow. Even if you're not a frequent traveler with built-up points, you certainly will become one in the course of taking this journey for yourself! Work with specific airlines, rental car companies, and hotel branches, and sign up for their customer loyalty programs—it doesn't take long to start earning rewards!

Look around your life and consider the benefit programs you're involved in. Baseball is a big business, and teams often partner with other large brands to drive up attendance and get you better deals. Credit card companies often have cards with cash back bonuses, or cards that will earn you extra rewards points towards your interests. Several banks even offer baseball-specific cards, where every dollar you spend on them earns you points you can redeem for MLB game tickets and memorabilia.

Many employers also team with MLB teams in their area, and might offer discounts, free tickets, or access to club level seating—go to your H.R. department and ask if there's anything special. Many stadiums have specific discount evenings for various careers and special interests. Insurance programs like AAA and USAA frequently offer deals and discounts that can be applied at baseball games and for general travel expenses. The Internet is full of coupon programs and special rates for hotels, restaurants, and travel. Just because the sticker price looks high doesn't mean you should be discouraged! Always look around for deals, it will significantly decrease the expense.

It was important to us to use this journey as a teaching experience for our children. We went to a lot of museums and historical sites, and participated in other activities, and we incorporated fun and educational side trips along the way. First and foremost, we always wanted this to be a great experience for them, a really fun memory that they would want to share with their own families someday.

From the start, we wanted to involve them in the planning process as well, to make the trip about the entire family. We would ask them to pick out the game or stadium that was most important for them to see each season, and this helped us determine where to start. They made the decisions from their hearts, and told us who they were dreaming about going to see. After we had that baseline, we would start suggesting other activities in the area, things we wanted to do and see, like Niagara Falls in New York, the Liberty Bell in Philadelphia, and horseback riding in Kentucky. Niagara Falls was a particularly exciting stop. We took a ride on the *Maid of the Mist* boat that approaches the Falls and got thoroughly soaked. We highly recommend trying it! Philadelphia was wonderful as well, and we talk about our time there elsewhere in the book. Since we've always been big sports fans, we'd always try to hit sports museums as well, like the Hockey Hall of Fame or Football Hall of Fame, and other interesting museums along the way, like the Rock and Roll Hall of Fame. They learned a ton while having a great time.

We also involved them in the budgeting process to learn about the costs, because we wanted them to be aware, financially, of what was involved. It was really helpful for them to have that background. This was especially important with Dayna's financial background and Steve's keen eye for budgeting. They didn't know every single detail about the planning; we didn't want to burden them down with all of that, it was more about fun and picking up tricks and tips. If we were going to a Hall of Fame, they would be close by, listening while Steve would buy the tickets, and they'd learn to ask about pricing and discounts. They would learn a little bit more about finance with each trip because we were trying to budget. As they got older, they were put in charge of their own budgets at the gift stores for each stadium, and they would get to make their own decisions, knowing they had a private budget per stadium. Jack actually did a project for school to see how much a family vacation costs, and chose to do it on our Toronto trip; he plugged in the airfare to Toronto, ballgame costs, hotel costs, and prices for the Hockey Hall of Fame and food. It was a fantastic, practical, and educational project.

Even though the experience of planning and budgeting for all the elements of these big trips isn't as exciting as actually being on them, some forethought can really make the entire experience much smoother and more enjoyable. We learned a lot along the way, and taught the boys some valuable lessons, so all in all, we really feel like we hit a grand slam!

CHAPTER SIX
Field of Dreams

Baseball culture runs very deep in North America, and there are many wonderful places to explore baseball history apart from the stadiums themselves. We tried to put effort into seeing the sights in the various cities we visited, and also attempted to hit the best hotspots between stadiums. Since we were already putting time and money into traveling across the country to visit all the ballparks, half the work was already done! We decided as a family to incorporate a mix of baseball and other stops along the way. Two of our favorite stops fell into the former category: the original filming location for *Field of Dreams* and the Louisville Slugger Museum.

We were fortunate enough to make it to the site of the film during its twenty-fifth anniversary year, in the summer of 2014. We were well into our adventure by then, and had decided to make our visit while traveling from a Royals game in Kansas City to the All-Star Game, to be held at Target Field in Minneapolis, Minnesota. The film location was in Dyersville, Iowa. At the time, the boys hadn't actually seen the film yet, so we planned ahead and ordered a copy, and had it sent to the hotel we would be staying at the night before the visit.

Baseball fans are all familiar with the Chicago White Sox and the Boston Red Sox, but what about the Black Sox? In 1919, the White Sox were facing the Cincinnati Reds in the World Series. Some of the Chicago players had been growing increasingly frustrated with Charles Comiskey, the owner, over salaries. These players thought they were not being paid nearly enough. They were legally bound to these low wages by their contracts, and felt the whole situation was unjust. Eventually some of the players got together and, under the leadership of first baseman Chick Gandil, conspired to work with gambling establishments to throw the series and get rich. He met with people in the gambling scene, and set the plan in motion.

They did end up throwing the series and getting the money, but they had not covered their tracks well enough to get away with it. A grand jury was convened in 1921 after Comiskey, inundated with rumors of corruption within his club, suspended eight players suspected of the fraud. It didn't take long for all eight to be found guilty, and they suffered punitive fines. In addition, all eight players were banned for life from major league play.

One of the eight, "Shoeless" Joe Jackson, happened to be one of the strongest players of the era. Indeed, he still holds a number of team hitting records from his time on the White Sox and Indians. If he hadn't forfeited his eligibility for induction into the Hall of Fame by being banned, he would certainly be there now alongside contemporaries and friends like Babe Ruth and Ty Cobb. He passed away in 1951, and there remains significant doubt as to his actual involvement in the scandal. He maintained his innocence until the end, and many fans hope that the ban will be reversed and he will come into his true baseball legacy.

Field of Dreams has become one of our favorite family movies since we first watched it together on the trip. It tells the story of Ray Kinsella (played by Kevin Costner), a struggling farmer who one night hears a voice whisper to him from his cornfields, "If you build it, he will come." After hearing the voice several more times, he momentarily sees a baseball diamond instead of his fields. He decides to trust the voice, and razes the corn to build a baseball field. Sometime later, he glances out his window and sees a man in an outdated baseball uniform in the diamond, and goes down to speak to him. The man claims to be Joe Jackson himself (played by Ray Liotta), and he is very happy to be on the baseball diamond again. He asks Ray if he can bring a few more players, and soon the other seven players banned in 1921 are back again, playing the game they loved so much. There are more twists, turns, and time travel hijinks in the film that we won't get into here! We encourage you to watch it; it is a beautiful film that has a great message for everyone. It tells us that youthful innocence and the joy of the game can triumph over tragedy and lost chances. After seeing it, the boys could barely contain their excitement at the thought of getting to see the film location and had hopes of running through the cornfield.

There are plenty of ways to keep kids occupied in the car on a long trip, as all parents know. Some favorite ways of passing the time for us were keeping an eye out for all fifty state license plates, I Spy With My Little Eye, and the punch-bug game...but it can get out of hand from the driving dad's perspective! Obviously baseball is ever a popular topic, and the boys were still talking about the film, and various games we had seen that summer. As time goes on and the boys get older, iPads and iPhones can be a huge help passing time in the car while traveling from stadium to stadium.

As we began to approach the field, the excitement from the boys in the back of the car was palpable. Before quite reaching the Field of Dreams, Steve stopped the car at the end of the road prior to the entrance, and we let Jack and Grant run the rest of the way. The boys described the feeling like running from the bullpen to pitch the final out. After being cooped up in the car for over five hours, and in the middle of a particularly exciting period of our baseball journey, they sure needed it! They sprinted down the long dirt road, through the corn, and straight to the diamond, gloves in hand.

The site of the film has been maintained as a tourist attraction since the film came out in 1989. In preparation for the anniversary, everything had been spruced up and cleaned, and it looked just like in the movie apart from the large wooden sign identifying the field. As it happened, we weren't the only baseball fans who had come up with the idea to visit during that special year. While the kids were running around, we bumped into a man by the name of Ed Hearn. He is not only a retired MLB player, but had played in the World Series for the New York Mets in 1986. He had also written a fantastic memoir in the 90s, *Conquering Life's Curves*, and was gracious enough to sign copies of it for the boys. This would make for an excellent addition to the collection of autographs! For them, the day kept getting better and better, as they were soon trying on his World Series ring, and receiving valuable pitching tips from a veteran of the game, all of it happening on a famous baseball landmark. He had also brought his World Series trophy with him, and the boys got to take a picture holding it up. He was incredibly friendly and made our visit as magical as the movie. We never could have known that we would have these sorts of experiences, but the surprise twists and turns were always welcome, and made our journey something unique.

It was a wonderful experience. At one point the boys mentioned it was like being in heaven, and Mom and Dad quickly joked, quoting from the movie, "No, we are in Iowa!" We finished off by browsing in the small gift shop and playing hide and seek in the corn until it started to get dark. As the sun began to set we piled back into the car to continue on to our next hotel, the Hotel Julien Dubuque. Our next stop was going to be Target Field in Minneapolis for the All-Star Game, and we needed to be well rested to prepare for the upcoming days!

So far we have talked about the turf, wall height, weather conditions, and other elements that impact a game of baseball. There is another very important factor, and that is the equipment used. The materials, style, and proportions of a bat or ball change the dynamic of play. In addition to the practical effect equipment has on the game, there is a certain amount of emotional resonance attached to gear. There is a nostalgia that is associated with the well-worn leather glove, and the traditions involved in breaking it in. Balls that were hit for famous home runs are prized collectors' items, and others, like the ball used during the sixth game of the 1924 World Series thrown at the turn-back-the-clock game, are used in symbolic roles to add an historic touch to baseball events. The texture of the stitching on a ball, the smell of a leather glove, and weight of a wooden bat are part of the history of the game itself. This is one of the main reasons we love the Louisville Slugger museum. These baseball bats have been around for almost as long as professional play, and have a name-recognition unrivaled by any other brand of equipment in any other sport.

Louisville Slugger bats were first made in the late nineteenth century, when John Hillerich convinced his father, woodworker J. F. Hillerich, that there was going to be a market for baseball bats as the sport became more popular. The first run of bats was produced in the 1880s, and the line became the Louisville Sluggers we know today in the early 1890s. Their build quality was high, and the bats became incredibly popular. By the 1930s the company's standard bat was being used in professional baseball by countless Hall of Famers, record holders, and stars. Another interesting fact is that the Louisville Slugger was the first piece of sporting equipment to be endorsed by a professional player...something that is almost taken for granted today. Babe Ruth was one of several legends who officially endorsed the bats.

We visited the Louisville Slugger Museum for the first time in 2014. We were in the middle of a hectic portion of our trip, and couldn't stay for as long as we wanted. We vowed to visit again soon, and made it the next summer. Dayna's sister lives about an hour east of Louisville, in Lexington, Kentucky, and we were in town for Dayna's niece's wedding and decided to swing by the museum afterwards. It had been too perfect a side trip to pass up then, and we had a great time! From that first trip, the batting cages were the standout for Jack and Grant. You can only watch so much baseball without wanting to pick up a bat, glove, or ball, and play yourself!

It is easy to tell at first glance what the museum and factory are all about, as the outside of the building features a massive baseball bat that towers over the structure and appears to be leaning against the wall. At 120 feet tall and weighing 68,000 pounds, it is the largest bat in the world! Once inside, fans are treated to a feast of baseball history. One fascinating exhibit features profiles of famous players along with replicas of their

Slugger of choice. There are lifelike mannequins of players in mid-swing, their Sluggers in hand. And at the top of the popularity charts, an actual Louisville Slugger used by Babe Ruth, with which he broke the seasonal home run record (59) in 1927. His record would stand for over thirty years, until another Louisville-toting power hitter, Roger Maris, popped sixty-one balls over the fence in 1961. Seeing this bat, beautifully preserved in a sealed display case, was awe-inspiring! The museum is interesting, but so is the factory; we got to see some bats being made, including pink bats used by many players at Mother's Day games! This tradition started several years ago, and many players that we have gotten to watch and meet have brandished them, like Albert Pujols, Torii Hunter, and Coco Crisp.

The history of the baseball bat is long and complex, and we hope you check out some of books in our bibliography to find out more. Babe Ruth's bat is made of hickory, which was used for a long time due to its availability and hardness. For many decades, ash was the most widely used; players valued its strength and lightness, which made it easy and forgiving to swing. Nowadays the vast majority of players use maple bats, a trend that became popular in the 1990s. Maple is an incredibly hard wood that has very little give. Since it is so hard, it imparts a ton of force when striking a ball. Most of the heaviest hitting sluggers of contemporary baseball have used maple bats, including Barry Bonds. There are a few who use birch as well, as it strikes a balance between the benefits of maple and ash, being lighter than the former and harder than the latter.

We had finished the tour the previous summer, but had something special planned for this return trip to the museum. It took some effort to keep it secret, but since we knew we were going to come back to Louisville, we had planned a special gift. At the museum, we presented the boys with custom, engraved Louisville Sluggers that read, "We Hit 'Em All!" They were shocked! The beautiful bats are now on display in their rooms.

We were preparing to leave when we found out from a nice service person at the museum that the Louisville Bats team had a game later that day. The Bats are a minor league team, and the affiliate at the Triple-A level for the Cincinnati Reds. We had a few hours to spare before our flight home, so we decided to head over and watch the game. The Bats play at Louisville Slugger Field, a five-minute drive away from the museum and factory. It ended up being a pretty amazing stop. The game was great, and there were tons of little perks that made it the perfect way to say farewell to the area. There was a free lunch included with the purchase of a ticket, and you could choose from hamburgers, hotdogs, and other classic ballpark foods. They were also giving away visors with the stadium and Bats' logos on them. Another fantastic surprise!

The Louisville Slugger Museum was one of the best that we have ever been to. During this trip we visited with Aunt Doe, and the boys got to improve their horseback-riding skills at the Kentucky Horse Park in Lexington. It is a wonderful park, and a must-see for horse lovers. Dayna's niece was married at the beautiful Keeneland Racecourse, a historic thoroughbred racing course that has been hosting important competitions for more than seventy-five years. Keeneland is just a short drive from the Kentucky Horse Park, and we recommend them both.

We have shared with you quite a few team and region specific museums that we enjoyed, but there are several more that stand out. One of these was the Sports Legends Museum at Camden Yards, right next to the Orioles Park at Camden Yards in Baltimore, Maryland. As mentioned elsewhere in our book, the original Orioles moved from Baltimore to New York, where they eventually became the Yankees, around a hundred years ago. The current Baltimore Orioles spent a season as the Milwaukee Brewers at their inception in 1901, and then played as the St. Louis Browns for fifty-two years before coming to rest in Baltimore as the new Orioles.

Camden Yards is a beautiful and important stadium, and should be high on the list of parks to see for those interested in sports architecture and history. Several of the stadiums we have mentioned (such as Busch Stadium and PNC Park) have a pronounced, retro architectural style that calls to mind the ballparks of the late 1800s and early 1900s. These parks all feature exposed steel, prominent brickwork, and brightly colored seating. They were all inspired by the park in Camden Yards, which opened to the public in 1992.

Even though he never played for the Orioles (well, not until they had been the Yankees for many years!), Babe Ruth is a part of Baltimore baseball history, and he grew up just a short distance from where they play today. He was born George Herman Ruth, Jr., in 1895 in the city, and spent his early years with his family on Goodyear Street. Memorial Park, the Orioles stadium that preceded Camden Yards, would be built after his death very close by, and even be known informally as "Babe Ruth Stadium."

Both Babe Ruth and the Orioles were honored in the Sports Legends Museum, which in late 2015 closed its doors permanently after a disagreement over terms of the lease. When we visited in 2012, it was a great museum, and featured an impressive collection of memorabilia from many different sporting traditions. Baseball fans should not give up hope, however, as much of the Babe Ruth collection was transferred to the Babe Ruth Birthplace Museum, which is located at 216 Emory Street. This is the house in which Babe Ruth was born, and is just a few blocks from the Orioles' park. Baseball history buffs will be able to find The Babe's jerseys, and an impressive collection of rare photographs and video footage of the legend.

Back to Camden Yards! It is a phenomenal stadium, and it is no surprise that so many teams took design cues from it. The front is very stately, and boasts that famous red brick. Once inside, fans can treat themselves to plenty of local food, the best of which highlights Maryland's seafood tradition. Rather than have a centralized area dedicated to team history, the Orioles have chosen to pepper the whole park with interesting nods to the Birds of the past. One can spot retired jerseys and championship pennants throughout the stadium, and check out the Orioles Hall of Fame on a wall past centerfield. When we were visiting, a statue garden was being constructed. There were only a few statues a few years ago, but it has since been expanded considerably.

One of the largest exhibits we saw commemorated the career of Pete Rose, and was in Cincinnati, at the Reds' museum. Pete Rose played for the Reds from 1963 to 1978, and was the recipient of many awards. One of his accomplishments is the all-time hit record of 4,236 hits. 4,236 baseballs, each representing one hit in Rose's career, were displayed behind glass, stretching up more than three floors. Some of them were marked out as significant, like the 1,000th, 2,000th, and so on. Others that stood out included the 2,881st hit, which broke the record for switch hitters, and the 3,035th hit, which kicked off Rose's forty-four game hitting streak in 1978. Seeing them all together in one place was impressive, and our hats are off to the staff that put it all together.

It was also very cool to see Johnny Bench's exhibit in the Reds' museum. Bench was invited to the All-Star game over a dozen times, and won the World Series twice with the Reds. He is often considered one of the greatest catchers in history. He was also quite a slugger, and in two different years he was both National League home run leader *and* winner of a Golden Glove for outstanding fielding!

The Cardinals have one of the largest museums that we visited. One of our favorite restaurants at a ballpark was the Cardinal Nation, and right above it was the museum. They have a "Holding History" area, where it is possible to try on jerseys and swing bats that players on the team once used; you get to pick one of five different players from Cardinals history and get your picture taken holding their bat. Steve borrowed a jersey from someone in line for his picture, but the kids were prepared.

In New York, we were able to see the FAO Schwartz Toy Store before it closed. At the time it was the largest toy store in the world, and had been for over 145 years. There was a big display promoting *Smurfs 2* that the boys got a kick out of. One of the coolest things about New York was the double-decker bus tour that we took. It hit a lot of important sites that we were glad the boys could see: Wall Street, the National September 11 Memorial and Museum, and the view of the Statue of Liberty. They even got to announce some of the sights on the microphone system for the rest of the tour! And, of course, we had to play whiffle ball in Central Park.

We went to some usual tourist attractions as well, like the Grand Canyon. This ended up being an eventful trip in more ways than one! But before heading to the Grand Canyon we saw our first game at the Arizona Diamondbacks' stadium, Chase Field.

This was one of the stadiums that we had time to tour before the game. We were staying right across the street at the Westin, but the stadium does have its own metro stop, so it is easily accessible almost no matter where you are staying in the city. The Diamondbacks are the youngest team in the major leagues, and were founded in 1998. Chase Field has been their home the whole time, and is a great place to catch a game. From the outside it appears as a clean mixture of cool greens and greys, set against the deep blue Arizona sky and dusty Arizona earth. Phoenix makes the news each year for breaking some temperature record or another, so we thought that one of the coolest features, literally, was the swimming pool off the right-centerfield fence. The area with the pool can be rented out for a high price tag, but we are sure there is nothing like relaxing in the pool while food is served, waiting for a fly ball!

Also on the tour we saw the World Series trophy, from when the D'backs had won a few years ago. It was certainly impressive for the team to win the World Series, over the Yankees no less, less than ten years after they became a team. Chase Field was good to them that year, and they won all four games at home to take the Championship. We were surprised to learn that the retractable roof can go from fully closed to fully opened in a matter of three minutes, quite a bit faster than other stadiums like Safeco.

After the game, we drove to Sedona, a beautiful town outside Flagstaff nestled amongst incredible red sandstone structures. The landscape is very unique there, and we took one of the famous Pink Jeep tours to really soak it all in. We all piled into one of the jeeps and took off into the buttes and mountains, four-wheeling over the rocky terrain. It was very exciting and worth the trip!

Our hotel was much closer to the Grand Canyon itself, which we got to see shortly after. One of the hotels next to us, that we would love to stay at on a return trip, is the El Tovar. It has a very interesting history, as it is one of the oldest structures in the area still in use. It was built in 1905, when the area was still largely untamed, and has seen many famous guests, including President Theodore Roosevelt. Grant lost his first tooth that night, an exciting event that would quickly be overshadowed by the gigantic Arizona elk that were on the front lawn when we woke up!

Chicago was another very packed trip, both for baseball and conventional site-seeing. This was much later, in 2013, when we could schedule time to see both the Cubs and the White Sox. We took the Chicago Cruise Line tour, which focused on the truly amazing architecture of the city. Chicago at the turn of the century was one of the most important cities in the country. It had just hosted the Columbian Exhibition in 1893, beating out New York and Washington D.C., and many of the important buildings on the tour date to that era (the Cubs were formed around the same time, in 1900). Later on we had pizza at the famous Pizzeria Uno. Steve had had pizza there many years before as a child visiting the city with his parents, and it is just as good now. The lines were long, but the meal was worth it. We took the subway to see both the White Sox and the Cubs, something the boys always enjoy.

Wrigley and Fenway have a special place in the annals of baseball history. They are the oldest stadiums still in use, and have seen too many historic moments to count. We loved Wrigley, and the timelessness that it still brings, despite a number of modern additions, to the game of baseball. For one thing, Wrigley was the first stadium to have an organized concessions system, and the ice cream stand that we got some treats at is one of the oldest in the major leagues. Food elsewhere in the stadium was fantastic as well. Jack had a large portion of nachos...in a batting helmet! It is an impressive amount of food, but you get a nice souvenir out of it.

Wrigley Field has a long and complicated history. The Cubs are another team that played under various names in the late 19th century. In 1907 they became the Cubs, and some years later they came under the control of entrepreneur Charles Weeghman. Shortly after acquiring the team, he began constructing a new stadium. It opened in the spring of 1914, and was called Weeghman Park.

Financial ups and downs pulled control of the team away from Weeghman over the next few years, and stakes in the team were bought up by William Wrigley, the man behind the Wrigley chewing gum company. By

1921 he owned the entire franchise, and renamed the stadium. It would be renovated several times over the years. The history and lore associated with Wrigley Field and the Chicago Cubs is rivaled by very few teams, and they figure as one of the most important pieces of baseball culture.

The first time the boys ever rode a train was from New York City to Boston, an experience we highly recommend. That was an event unto itself, and ever since, they have loved public transportation of all kinds. It doesn't hurt that this works pretty well for Mom and Dad as well! We stayed at a very nice hotel, the Courtyard in Copley Square, next to Newberry Street in Boston. One of the tours we would like to mention that we took in Boston is another aquatic one—the well-known Boston Duck tour. The tour itself is on a very cool vehicle, a World War II era amphibious landing craft, modified with some nice seats and a coat of bright yellow paint. The tour was very fun and informative! The tour guides were very accommodating and interactive, like those on the bus tour of New York City, and let the boys steer the boat and announce one or two sights along the way. We stayed at a hotel close to the stadium. Another neat thing to do in Boston are the tandem bike self-tours. Your group can rent a few tandem bikes, and get a detailed itinerary for a tour of the city. The bikes were *much* harder to use than we thought! It takes quite a bit of coordination to get them going and to maintain a good speed. Eventually we got into the swing of things and pedaled our way past M.I.T. all the way to Harvard, where we had lunch, and back.

When it comes to Boston, one of the first things that comes to mind is the baseball tradition. Fenway and the Red Sox are emblematic of the baseball tradition in North America, and the Boston fans are some of the loudest, most loyal of them all. We made it to Fenway at about the halfway point in our trip, in 2011. It was a magical experience. We touched the aforementioned Green Monster, sang "Sweet Caroline" at the bottom of the eighth, and got autographs from a few former players and coaches in front of the park. Some of the streets are blocked off, and then filled with game-going fans...it feels like a baseball carnival, and for some, is the quintessential American baseball experience.

After all this baseball history, with its twists and turns, moving teams and stadium turnover, you might be surprised to know that one team has been located in the same city, and has had the same name, for over 120 years: the Philadelphia Phillies. They have been around since 1883, and have a unique tie to the city that many other teams don't have. Unfortunately, this means that the Phillies have also lost more games than any other major league team, but that doesn't faze them much. In fact, a couple of Philadelphia radio show hosts celebrated the Phillies' 10,000th loss by dumping 10,000 marbles down the steps of the Philadelphia Art Museum in 2007. Losses or no losses, though, Philadelphia loves its baseball.

Getting to their game against the Braves was probably the easiest time we had on our whole trip, since the hotel we were staying at, a Holiday Inn, was right across the street. Citizens Bank Park was built in 2004 to replace Veterans Stadium (another multi-use stadium; this one also was home to the Philadelphia Eagles football team). Because the Phillies have so much history in the area, there are many places to check out interesting exhibits commemorating past players. The most prominent of these is Ashburn Alley, an area located behind center field. Here you can find exhibits honoring Phillies All-Stars and Hall of Famers, as well as a bunch of interactive games. The boys love baseball and its history, but sometimes they just need to unwind and play a game. One of the coolest was a carnival-like game where fans can run in place to power their way along a large field up on the wall. You can win prizes at some of these games, and Ashburn Alley is usually a popular place for families to relax over the course of a busy baseball day.

We actually got off to a slow start, as the game was delayed by rain for a little bit. But like most of the downsides to our trip, there was a silver lining, and we took that time to try out what ended up being a fantastic restaurant in the stadium, McFadden's. Michael Bourn, centerfielder for the Braves, alone made that game a great one! He had just been named to the All-Star team, and showed that this was a deserved honor by hitting, scoring, and stealing bases on his way to a 6 to 3 victory for his team over the Phillies. Citizens is a great park, with great food and a great mascot! The Phillie Phanatic is probably one of the funniest, most interactive mascots we have seen on all of our trips. Some mascots stick around the playing field or the lower levels, but some like the Pittsburgh Parrot and the Phanatic take their antics all through the stadium. He is green, funny looking, and the kids rave about him.

Philadelphia is a wealth of baseball history, but it also stands out as one of the oldest major cities in the U.S. and offers a wealth of historic sites and artifacts to check out. We made an educational side trip during our stay to the historic district and saw the Liberty Bell, which is an easy recommendation for those with or without families. There is so much to see in the city of Philadelphia!

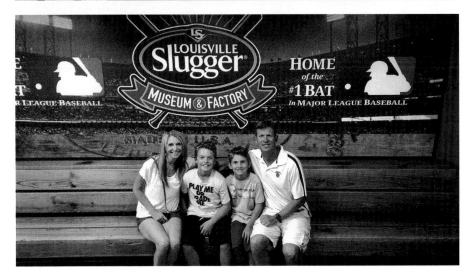

CHAPTER SEVEN

Cactus League

Like so many other baseball traditions, spring training is an old but ever-developing one! Traveling south and west to play during the chilly winter months in the Northeast is almost as old as professional play. Before the days of covered, climate-controlled ballparks, clubs would flee northern regions to go on southern tours, playing in cities like Savannah and Augusta, Georgia, or even heading down to Mexico and Cuba. As leagues became more organized and seasons more standardized, these winter getaways were shortened into training sessions in the spring. The oldest regularly used spring training stadium, McKechnie Field, is nearly as old as Fenway, and opened in 1923. This has been our Pittsburgh Pirates' training ground for many years, and Roberto Clemente, among others, practiced there. Professional teams have played against private teams, college teams, and more during spring training over the years, and eventually the system became what it is today.

We have had many wonderful experiences during spring training, and love attending exhibition games. Teams prefer training in warmer climates, and over the years have formed two leagues, organized by region. The East Coast league is known as the Grapefruit League, and plays in Florida. The highest concentration of facilities for this league runs from Tampa to Orlando, and a road trip laterally through central Florida could net you exhibition games at half a dozen stadiums. We have been based in San Diego for a number of years now, so we most frequently see exhibition games in the Cactus League, active in Arizona. The facilities are a bit closer together in the Cactus League, clustered mostly around Phoenix.

We highly recommend the Cactus League spring training experience. The teams are split evenly at this point between Cactus League and Grapefruit League, and catching spring training in both areas has many appeals!

Grapefruit League Teams	Cactus League Teams
Atlanta Braves	Arizona Diamondbacks
Baltimore Orioles	Chicago Cubs
Boston Red Sox	Chicago White Sox
Detroit Tigers	Cincinnati Reds
Houston Astros	Cleveland Indians
Miami Marlins	Colorado Rockies
Minnesota Twins	Kansas City Royals
New York Mets	Los Angeles Angels of Anaheim
New York Yankees	Los Angeles Dodgers
Philadelphia Phillies	Milwaukee Brewers
Pittsburgh Pirates	Oakland Athletics
St. Louis Cardinals	San Diego Padres
Tampa Bay Rays	San Francisco Giants
Toronto Blue Jays	Seattle Mariners
Washington Nationals	Texas Rangers

The split between Grapefruit League and Cactus League has a big impact on players who are traded. Troy Tulowitzki joked in an interview recently that going from the Cactus League to the Grapefruit League was like going from a country club to a more old-school facility, sparking an intense debate amongst fans and players alike. He had just been traded from the Colorado Rockies to the Toronto Blue Jays, and would have to make the move from Arizona to Florida. Many older players still fondly remember the many rougher spring training facilities they attended as young players, and hearing those stories is quite entertaining!

Exhibition stadiums don't vary as much as the big ones do, but each still has its own quirks and character. The largest and newest spring training facility in both the Cactus and Grapefruit Leagues is Sloan Park in Mesa, Arizona (Cactus League), where the Chicago Cubs play, and it seats over 14,000. The oldest spring training facility in the Cactus League is the HoHoKam Stadium, also in Mesa, which was built in 1964; the oldest spring training stadium in the Grapefruit League is McKechnie Field, which was built in Bradenton in 1923! Many of the stadiums are much newer, but some date back decades; as such, amenities, features, and concessions vary just as much as size.

Incorporating trips to spring training camps during your journey is well worth it for any baseball fan! Of course, regular season games provide higher stakes and more excitement, and you usually will not see any record-breaking performances, but spring training does offer a unique set of experiences for you and your family to enjoy. To begin with, the crowds are quite a bit smaller! This makes the experience more intimate, which is great if you are going to see your favorite team train and want the chance to meet some players. The tickets are also inexpensive at most of the stadiums, and we can't stress enough what a great value exhibition games are. You can easily find tickets right behind home plate for less than half the price of a seat not as close to the action during the regular season. While more relaxed than other professional sports, a live baseball experience isn't without its shoulder bumping, long lines, and parking battles. Spring training features much less of all these elements, which means everything will be just a little bit easier and less hectic.

Spring training itself is comprised of both practice sessions and actual exhibition games. Both are generally open to fans, but the former offer a better opportunity to snag an autograph. There are a number of websites that keep track of the open workout schedules for all the major league teams, so running into players getting on and off buses and relaxing between training sessions is very manageable.

We have been able to sit right behind the coaches on occasion, within earshot. You can tell, just from the way they talk about the game, that it isn't as competitive; everyone is here to grow their skills and practice for the upcoming season, which can be very inspiring to see. At the same time, these are high stakes for minor league players, young players, and players coming off the disability list to show off their best stuff and earn a spot on the team, so you'll often see some fantastic plays! Often times a team won't play their starting pitcher, or he will just pitch one inning. When we were at Talking Stick, there was a lot of buzz around the stadium because Zack Greinke was scheduled to start. He did, but he only pitched one inning. Usually the coaches don't want to tax starters, and Greinke probably just needed a warm up and then some time to rest his arm. After all, he does have a $206 million arm! You will definitely see some players get more time though, it all depends. For hitters, coaches often mess around with the batting order to find the right configuration, for example, so you might see a star like Pujols play for five innings or so. Spring training is a great place to see up-and-coming players try to prove themselves, and it was in this capacity that we got to see players like Kris Bryant, Trevor Story, and more at the start of their careers. In fact, Grant was lucky to be bat boy for the Rockies during spring training, just a few weeks before Story broke Willie Mays' record for most home runs over the first six games of the season. We were cheering hard when we saw him hit that seventh home run!

This system actually works out great for us, the fans! We love seeing a bunch of different players have their chance at the mound, and it makes the game more exciting because the new players are trying to impress everyone and earn a spot on the team during the regular season. One of the aspects of this less competitive play is that the final score doesn't really matter; if it has been a back-and-forth struggle and the teams end the ninth inning with an 8 to 8 score, they usually just walk off. No extra innings are played most of the time. You are going to see great players play a great game, but sometimes a tie can be anti-climactic, if those particular coaches and managers don't plan on forcing a result.

During spring training you can witness a lot of home runs! One game we saw, the one that ended in an 8 to 8 tie, was at one point a 5 to 1 game because of the number of home runs. Those young and untested pitchers who are trying to earn their places on the team are usually easy to spot, and experienced batters know how to take advantage of that. The games are often so high-scoring because there is a greater potential for error when starters aren't on the field. They are all amazing players, but at that point in the year, everyone is working out the kinks in their game, and some might not be as experienced as others. Don't go anywhere if the score is lopsided and the team you are rooting for is down. Anything can happen at spring training!

The Salt River Fields at Talking Stick stadium complex, which the Arizona Diamondbacks and Colorado Rockies call "home," is one of the nicest ones, both for players and fans, and one of our family favorites to hit up for spring training events. This is the first MLB stadium constructed on Native American land. The community in the region, the Salt River Pima-Maricopa Indian Community, won the right to build the stadium, in an attempt to boost the economic strength of the region. The complex has a number of fields and training areas, some of which are unusual and aren't generally seen outside of spring training. These include runs of infield dirt dedicated to sliding practice, a pitching machine area dedicated to bunting practice, and more. For the baseball-obsessed, this complex is a great place to see the nitty-gritty elements that go into preparations for the coming season. It is also a great place to bring large groups, and Dayna has led an opening week event for clients of her company there for several years. That early in the spring training season the energy level of Phoenix is very high, and combined with a state of the art facility like Talking Stick, you have the perfect recipe for a retreat.

The designers of Salt River realized that attending spring training was becoming more common with fans, so they incorporated a number of very nice features into the design that appeal to us as well. The main field, where the exhibition games are played, seats 11,000, and guests can treat themselves to raised restaurant-style seating, valet parking, perfect berm seating, and food that rivals that of many regular season stadiums. They even have vendors that stroll the aisles offering chocolate-covered strawberries on a stick! We definitely recommend it!

We have personally noticed that spring training is growing in popularity. The stadiums are getting larger, the food is getting better, and the state tourism agencies have realized that traveling baseball fans spend a lot of money while visiting for exhibition games! As a result, hotel reservations tend to go quickly. It is a good idea to book hotel rooms at least two or three months in advance. Another tip we have is to grab the Arizona KEY spring training guide. It can be found at stadiums, and even many hotels in the area. It has everything you need; history, schedules, bios of players and coaches, maps, and more! One final tip is to purchase the team media guide, if available, in each team's shop. With these reference materials in hand, you will be ready to make the most of your trip!

Because the games are so much more relaxed, many things happen that you would never see at a regular season game. Players sometimes will do their sprints in the outfield, for example, which you will *never* see during a regular season game. You will also see a lot of unique drills that you don't usually see during warm ups before a regular season game. For example, sometimes teams will get together their roster of catchers to practice blocking drills, or to practice the throw from home to second base to keep a base from being stolen. It is worth it to stay late to see these kinds of drills. Sometimes even crazier things happen!

Most of the advice we have already given holds for spring training exhibition games as well. Get there early, and stay late! You will have more chances than usual to get a player's attention during warm up, or after the game. The stakes aren't as high as they are during the regular season, to say nothing of the postseason, so players tend to be more laid back and open to engaging with fans. Teams also tend to run rookies in exhibition games, to get a sense of where they are at before the regular season starts. This might give you the chance to see up-and-coming players at the beginning of their careers, make connections before they hit the big time and are constantly swarmed by fans, and even get a signed rookie card.

What makes baseball so special is that you get to know the person next to you, and this holds true particularly at spring training. We are not saying you will become best friends, but people are open to talking. We sat down next to a few older folks at various games over the years, and had some great conversations. Jack even got asked once or twice for his autograph, since he had been playing in tournaments in the local area! Fans at games tend to befriend one another and band together.

The feeling is one of communal enjoyment and excitement. If there is a foul ball, for example, the person running that line will often grab the ball while it is still on the field. You can actually see the development of the crowd; they will get excited first at that wonderful sound of bat striking ball, then be a tad disappointed when it goes foul. The excitement creeps right back in quickly though, as soon fans are calling to the linesman, "Please, can we have the ball!" The person will often toss the ball to someone, hopefully a little kid, and the rest of the crowd will clap! The fans love it when this sort of thing happens, and they will look and watch and celebrate someone else making the effort and catching a ball, or getting a ball tossed to them from the field. The game of baseball is relaxed and fun, but also interactive!

Exhibition games are certainly not without their excitement! We got to see both Kyle Blanks and Yonder Alonso hit amazing grand slams at the Padres' Peoria complex back when they were both playing first base for San Diego. Spring training is a wonderful way to feel more closely connected with your favorite teams and players!

Attending spring training games will also give you the chance to do things you probably wouldn't be able to when attending regular or post-season games. Before we went to see the Cardinals take on the Marlins in an exhibition game in Jupiter, we donated a certain amount to a charity that is close to our hearts, and won the chance to throw the opening pitch. The charity is a joint fund between the Cardinals and the Marlins, and gives support to Little League non-profits and promotes youth sports. There were five people who got to throw, and Grant represented our family. It was a sellout crowd, a more frequently growing occurrence as spring training grows in popularity with the fans. It was a fantastic experience for him, and a very unique memory, but it was still stressful! He threw a great pitch, and while he felt it wasn't a perfect strike, any umpire would have called it one. As a matter of fact, one of Bob Shaw's old assistant coaches (and a good friend of Steve's parents) was watching that pitch. Gene can be found at every spring training game at Roger Dean Stadium down by the dugout, helping kids and getting autographs of his own. He has been a key figure in Jupiter baseball for a long time, and is partially responsible for keeping Dante Bichette and Kevin O'Sullivan involved in the sport, as he was their coach. It was a big day for Jack as well, as he earned a spot as honorary bat boy for the game. He also managed to get several autographs throughout the day, including one from Jason Heyward, three time Golden Glove award winner and 2010 All Star, which he was particularly excited to have gotten in the dugout. Later on, Grant finished his own day off in style with a signature from Adam Wainwright, starting pitcher for St. Louis. Getting autographs from visible icons like these players is the sort of thing young, aspiring players will never forget. It is an experience unlike any other, to meet someone you have held in such high esteem and that you have seen perform incredible feats on television. Major league players are larger-than-life figures to young kids, and it is a dream come true for kids to meet them, talk to them, and get autographs from them.

Spring training practice is a very different experience from watching practices and warm ups before regular season games. It is much more intimate, as there is often nothing but a bit of chain link fence between fans and players. This is the time when you will find the players at their most relaxed and approachable. It is one of the best times to grab autographs and maybe even get a chance to talk to the players. On top of all this, there is no cost to attend. There isn't a game to watch, but you can still see world-class pitchers warming up and world-class hitters improving their form. You can even hear coaches offering advice and corrections. It is a chance to peek into the inner workings of a professional baseball team and get some great tips on your own game, and is something no baseball fan will want to miss. One thing to bear in mind, if you are planning on attending a practice session, is that you will usually have no choice but to get up early, as practices often finish before noon. Consider getting into the habit of getting up and out the door early during baseball season, and you won't miss a thing!

In some ways, it is easier for fans to prepare for spring training games than during the regular season. For one thing, you only really have to look at two general areas: Phoenix, Arizona, and Central Florida. There are a few outliers in Florida (for example, the Orioles train as far south as Ft. Lauderdale). If you are going to Phoenix, bear in mind that, even in February and March, it gets very hot in the middle of the day. Depending on where you're coming from, it might be a welcome chance for you to defrost! Most of the parks don't have covered seating, so try and bring some combination of hats and sunscreen. Bring plenty of water and snacks as well, and enjoy the luxury of doing so, as a few stadiums (like Hammond Stadium in Fort Myers) don't allow outside food. And if you feel you and your group have the energy reserves necessary, remember that you can actually squeeze in two games a day!

Where would baseball teams be without their mascots? Well, we wouldn't want to hazard a guess! We are always glad to see our favorites, and so many teams bring their mascots with them to spring training. After all, they need to stay in shape too! Although few think about it, mascots are athletes as well, who attend their own training sessions and classes and camps. You'd be shocked how much strength and agility is required to be a good mascot! The costumes are very heavy and hot, and running around, keeping up the energy in the stadium with acrobatics is not easy! Quite a few teams make a point on social media to highlight the efforts mascots expend making sure their teams are packed and ready to head south when the time is right. One exhibition stadium, Goodyear Ballpark, even has its own mascot, Zizzy, who is always happy to rub shoulders and wings with the big-leaguers. Goodyear, as a side note, also features one of the largest kid-friendly areas at spring training, and features a full whiffle-ball field.

Goodyear Ballpark, where the Cincinnati Reds and the Cleveland Indians play, also happens to be one of our favorite Cactus League stadiums. It is technically the closest spring training facility to San Diego, about a five-and-half-hour drive, so it is the perfect place for us to start a trip to the Cactus League events. It is also more remote, relatively speaking, from the rest of the stadiums in the Phoenix area, so it is a quiet place to get settled before experiencing the rest of the world-class exhibition games and training. We can pack everyone up, drive in the morning, get there in time for a game, and get easy, inexpensive tickets right away. It's perfect!

We actually had a funny moment during one of our most recent trips to Goodyear. We had checked in, and were heading over to the ballpark when Steve got a call from a friend of ours who told us that we should hurry over—there were way more people than usual, and something was clearly going on. So we went over and found out that the first 2,000 fans that day got a Joey Votto bobblehead. Of course, we love bobbleheads, but Votto is also a star, and we were especially huge fans after we saw him being so instrumental in keeping Homer Bailey's no-hitter intact! Well, we rushed over to the main gate with our tickets, and before they were scanned, Steve asked if there were any bobbleheads left. The woman scanning the tickets said, "No, we are all out!" For a short moment we stood still not knowing what to do until Steve and the boys came up with a great idea, so we pocketed our tickets and ran around to the other entrance. Sure enough, there were about twenty-five of them left at the lesser-used gate. We had remembered seeing a bunch of boxes at that gate earlier, and pieced together that the bobbleheads were being given out at both entrances. So let this be another lesson for you! There might be a lot of competition for giveaways, but don't give up! Try another approach and your patience might be rewarded. As they say, "Try, try, try again, and you will be rewarded!"

Another time, the year before, we were at Goodyear attending a night game between the Reds and the Dodgers. We were enjoying the beautiful weather, watching the game, and noticed a bit of a commotion down near the seats behind home plate. We went down to investigate, and it turned out that Tommy Lasorda, legendary Dodgers manager was watching the game. There was an usher who was letting kids down to the area in small groups between innings, to get an autograph and say hello. Jack and Grant were troopers and patiently waited until the seventh-inning stretch, when they got their chance to visit the iconic manager. We did notice he was nodding off a bit towards the end of the game! Mr.

Lasorda, after such a storied and accomplished career, you deserve a nap on occasion at the ballpark; you've earned so much more, it was great to catch a game with you!

Some of the teams with the loudest and most loyal regular season fan bases are the most popular at spring training as well. This is true for the Chicago Cubs in particular. Cubs' spring training games have been selling out before the Cactus League season even starts! Their facility, Sloan Park, is brand new and state of the art, so the Cubs have a lot of draw. Reviews praise the berm, the rooftop seating, the customer service—basically everything but the parking! We made it out for a trip to Sloan just in time to include a bit about it in this book. Grant got to be bat boy for the Reds on the road and experience Sloan from the dugout. It was another perfect day in Arizona, and almost every seat in the place was filled. We did see a baseball fan sporting a great shirt that we will have to hunt around for and add to our roster. It said, "Life begins when the season starts," and featured a huge baseball. Our sentiments exactly! It is always a wonderful feeling to settle into your seat after a winter of no baseball. While at Sloan, we definitely recommend taking a picture by the Wrigley backdrop, which is a great photo spot. It is a miniature version of part of Wrigley that makes you feel like you are at the famous ballpark. It is very cool, and people line up to get their pictures taken there. One more note about Sloan: since the team and stadium are so popular, expect higher ticket prices than you would elsewhere in the area.

The Giants tend to sell out as well these days, even though their tickets also tend to be more expensive than average. Their Scottsdale Stadium is very nice, and in a premium location as well. Interestingly, it is one of the older ones in the Cactus League, and has since undergone some serious renovations to bring it up to the level of the other facilities. We've also been to Hohokam, where the Oakland Athletics play. The Cubs were there before, and the A's were at Phoenix Municipal. The Cubs built their own new complex, Sloan, and the old one was taken over and renovated by the Athletics. The shifting of teams and locations and training facilities offers kind of a microcosm of the greater MLB world, where teams have moved quite a bit as well! We have had some amazing experiences at both these stadiums, which you will read about shortly!

Hohokam doesn't plan on being left behind, and has plenty of great features after the twenty-six-million-dollar renovation. It now boasts the largest Jumbotron display in the Cactus League. It is spectacular! Dayna noticed it right away because she does sports photography, and if a Jumbotron is not updated, photographic images will not be clear. She rejoiced! At twenty-nine feet high, it may pale in comparison to the big dogs in the regular season stadiums, but it is a tremendous screen and gets lots of love from fans. Like a lot of the other Cactus League stadiums, there is some great lawn seating. Be prepared, and bring a glove so you can snag one of the many home runs!

We have been to the Peoria Sports Complex as well, where our Padres play. This is one of the few spring training facilities in the Cactus League that hosts two teams, the other team being the Seattle Mariners. It is a very nice facility, and one of our favorite features is "autograph alley," a passageway from the practice facility to the stadium that allows fans get autographs from players on their way from one to the other. We will talk about these stadiums quite a bit later on. Spring training is one of the parts of the baseball world our family enjoys the most!

Some teams have quirky traditions that they practice only during spring training. Most of the Reds starters, after the fifth inning of an exhibition game, burst out of the dugout and exit all together through the centerfield tunnel, for example. It is pretty impressive because it looks like a sea of red when they move all at once. Grant actually joined them, when he was bat boy delivering water to umpires in centerfield, and was lost in the sea since he was wearing his own Reds uniform. It's great to be able to get to know the more playful, small details of the teams and see them at their most quirky before the season and the serious competition starts!

Spring training has also given us the chance to see a lot of retired players and Hall of Famers that we normally would never have gotten to see. Many teams invite these players to act as wandering instructional coaches, who will be on-hand during warmups and drills to offer advice and help players with their form. Some others are brought in just so they can see the game, which is always nice. There are also a lot of scouts, and the kids have a great time picking them out of the crowd by their speed guns! The scouts are out in full force during spring training, checking out the up-and-coming talent.

We were outside of Scottsdale Stadium one morning, and an SUV pulled up. Two gentlemen got out and one opened the passenger door, and we were stunned when Willie Mays himself stepped out. Mays needs no introduction, of course...suffice to say that with his two dozen All-Star appearances, numerous Golden Glove awards, fifth place on the all-time home run list, and more, quite a few people consider him the greatest baseball player in history. It was honor to see him, just four feet away, as he was escorted into the stadium to a respectful and admirable applause. A good friend that we will mention later, Kirk, has been to spring training games for many years, and can't even remember how many Hall of Fame players he has seen just wandering the ballparks during spring training. There is simply nothing that compares to an experience like this!

Spring training is a lot of fun, the perfect sort of relaxed supplement to the regular season. People are just happy that baseball is back. As we said earlier, it's the same game, the outcome just isn't as important. It doesn't matter, to the point that sometimes managers will do a split squad, which is dividing the starters and the B team in two, merge the halves, and have them play at the same time against other teams. Usually in the case of a split squad, the team will want to have the starters at their "home" stadium, though, so keep that in mind. If home fans have paid good money to watch the Reds play in their stadium, managers usually won't have a split squad when the stars are off playing somewhere else.

The kids have been really lucky to have several chances to be bat boys, due to both relationships that we have with some of the teams and a bit of good luck and kindness from "Clubhouse Heroes" behind the scenes. Sometimes, though, it is just a matter of being at the right place at the right time. For example, when we were at a game at Talking Stick, during two separate years, Grant just got randomly picked from the crowd. Afterwards, Steve went up and spoke to the intern in charge of picking bat boys for the game and expressed his appreciation. He also asked why Grant was picked, and got a great tip for the future. The reply was that usually interns go to the visitor side (in this case, the Athletics, since the home team was the Diamondbacks) and look for two kids that are about twelve years old. On that day, we had gotten there about an hour before the game to grab some autographs. We were down near the fence in our A's gear, and Grant certainly looked the part. The folks searching for bat boys look for kids who seem interested and presentable. Grant had a glove and the right attitude! The intern had asked Grant and his friend, "Hey, we are looking for two bat boys...you interested?" And that was that! It was another random, special moment that made all the difference in the world. You can imagine it is a special day when you can bat boy for the professionals with one of your best friends!

Kevin Millar and Chris Rose threw out the first pitch that game. Millar was well known to Grant because he is on *Intentional Talk*, a talk show on *MLB Network*, and is a former MLB player and World Series Champion. Millar is a great, funny guy, and had been going around grabbing interviews with players before the game. Rose is his co-host. Grant was on the field during the opening pitch, and got to give Millar a fist bump. The boys are big fans of the show, so that was a fun added bonus!

We have only been to one Grapefruit League game, the one where Grant got to throw out the opening pitch. We really hope to attend more in the future and "hit 'em all" for both spring training leagues. The locations are very different, and there are many more conventional attractions near the Florida facilities that offer great opportunities for a family trip. On top of that, the Grapefruit League is much older, and has a deeper history than the comparatively shiny and new Cactus League. Here is a list of some great things to do near the Grapefruit League stadiums that we hope to check out, and some of the neat features to look forward to. We hope you are able to check them out too!

Team	Stadium	Location (FL)	More Info
Atlanta Braves	Champion Stadium	Lake Buena Vista	-Located in Walt Disney World's Wide World of Sports Complex -Built in a unique Spanish Mission style -The only Grapefruit League stadium with a complete upper deck -Has played host to multiple Major League games and part of the 2006 World Baseball Classic
Baltimore Orioles	Ed Smith Stadium	Sarasota	-Completely renovated in 2011 in a Mediterranean style -Named after the late Ed Smith, former president of the Sarasota Sports Committee
Boston Red Sox	JetBlue Park	Fort Myers	-Became the Red Sox's new home after a move from City of Palms Park in 2012 -Designed with a mix of traditional Fenway-style details (including the park's own "green monster," complete with vintage hand-operated scoreboard) and modern Florida flair -Known to the team as "Fenway South" -"Sweet Caroline" played during 7th inning stretch (same as at Fenway Park)
Detroit Tigers	Joker Marchant Stadium	Lakeland	-Built in 1966 in a Mediterranean style, its poured concrete construction has stood the test of time -Part of the Tigertown complex -Named after Marcus "Joker" Marchand, Lakeland's one-time director of Parks and Recreation.
Houston Astros	Osceola County Stadium	Kissimmee	-Designed and built in 1985 by the same architecture firm responsible for Camden Yards in Baltimore -At only 5,300, official capacity it is the smallest spring training ballpark -"Deep in the Heart of Texas" played during 7th inning stretch (same as at Minute Maid Park)

Team	Stadium	Location (FL)	More Info
Miami Marlins, St. Louis Cardinals	Roger Dean Stadium	Jupiter	-The only Grapefruit League stadium to host two different ball clubs, the Cardinals since 1998 and Marlins since 2003 -Half of the stadium is Marlins themed, half is Cardinals themed -Named for local car dealer
Minnesota Twins	Hammond Stadium	Fort Myers	-Best feature may be its facade design, which was inspired by Churchill Downs, the annual home of the Kentucky Derby in Louisville, KY -Received a major renovation in 2014 and 2015
New York Mets	Tradition Field	Port St. Lucie	-Originally a gift from developer Thomas White -Tradition Field is home to a 9/11 memorial that includes a piece of steel from the World Trade Center
New York Yankees	Steinbrenner Field	Tampa	-Largest Grapefruit League stadium, with an official capacity of 11,076 -Much like the New York Mets' Tradition Field, Steinbrenner Field also plays host to a 9/11 memorial that includes a piece of the World Trade Center -Most interesting architectural feature is a series of panels spelling out "YANKEES" between the stadium's roof supports -Named for the Yankees' controversial former owner, the late George Steinbrenner
Philadelphia Phillies	Bright House Field	Clearwater	-Opened in 2004, Bright House Field has many amenities usually reserved for major league stadiums, including an open, wrap-around concourse and a full-service outfield tiki bar. -Exterior is a unique take on Spanish Mediterranean architecture

Team	Stadium	Location (FL)	More Info
Pittsburgh Pirates	McKechnie Field	Bradenton	-Nestled into a neighborhood in the city of Bradenton, the site of McKechnie Field has been home to baseball for over 90 years -Recently remodeled in 2003 -Spanish Mission style facade -Field hosted its first ever night game in 2008 after lights were finally installed
Tampa Bay Rays	Charlotte Sports Park	Port Charlotte	-Used to be home to the Texas Rangers during spring training, but after extensive renovations (which included a total reconstruction of the façade), the Rays moved in for the 2009 season -Highlights include the "Baseball Boardwalk," a large walkway in the outfield that houses a tiki bar
Toronto Blue Jays	FL Auto Exchange Stadium	Dunedin	-Tucked in near downtown Dunedin, the field is bordered by a school, library, VFW hall and local cafe -Smallest in actual spring training capacity, due to lack of standing room which allows the Astros' stadium to hold more fans -All interior surfaces are painted blue for the team
Washington Nationals	Space Coast Stadium	Viera	-Vinyl facade painted red, white, and blue for the Nationals -Stadium gets its name from the nearby Kennedy Space Center, and until 2013, a memorial to shuttle disasters adorned each foul pole

For our most recent spring training trip, we decided to do something special. Our family was accompanied by the roster of the La Costa Rebels, the 10U Pony League travel ball team that Jack plays for, where Steve is assistant coach. The logistics were a bit more complicated with lots of families, to be sure, but the payoff was worth it! The team trip was orchestrated by a good friend of ours, Kirk, who has been manager of the Rebels for several years. He is an old hand at both attending spring training and traveling with teams, having been to the Cactus League every spring for over twenty years. This makes his perspective a unique one, as he has seen the development of the facilities, and the transition of spring training from a small-scale enterprise to the full-blown, commercial baseball phenomenon that it is today.

We aren't the first to have brought a full team of our own to the Cactus League. As Kirk told us, March in Arizona is always an extremely busy time for baseball fans! There are tournaments for travel youth teams, and of course spring training and exhibition games. Quite a few youth teams will travel in groups to exhibition games in between their own contests, and we decided some months beforehand to give it a try. This is definitely something you want to plan and set up way in advance! Kirk was ready to grab the tickets for games when they went on sale, which is usually in late December or early January, and hotel reservations were made very shortly after that. Back in his day it was possible to stroll up to the ticket counter right before a game, pay ten bucks, get a ticket, and then feast on $2 beers and even cheaper hotdogs. Nowadays the facilities are state of the art, and much bigger. The crowds are much larger as well, so at many stadiums it is only possible to get tickets ahead of time. The same holds true for hotels; get your reservations in early, because they will fill up! Our Rebels weren't part of a tournament this particular year, but Kirk did set up a number of matches against other travel teams in the area. This way, the boys could scratch the playing and watching baseball itches at the same time! Another friend associated with the team, whom we affectionately call Big Kat, brought his massive RV as well. He likes to stick a sign in front that says, "Parking Reserved for La Costa Rebels," and the kids love it. With our "mascot" RV in attendance, we were ready to roll!

You will see some cool things that only happen at spring training. After a game, Jeff Kent, National League MVP, was doing his sprints. Kirk always took a team picture on the dugout after the game. Well, they were all posed, ready to take the pictures, when Kent came running over and jumped up to be in the picture! Grant was once photobombed by the catcher for the Reds, Tucker Barnhart, while being bat boy. Billy Hamilton is another one of the up and comers that always brings energy into the dugout for sure. He drops his gear after getting to the dugout, high fives his teammates, and walks directly over to the bat boys to give them high fives. He'll pose for pictures readily, and is very friendly. He loves to make sure the bat boys feel like part of the team. Experiencing this kind of connection with a star player is a great thrill.

On our Rebels' team trip, our first big stop was Sloan Park, where later in the day we would see the Cubs and the Reds face off in front of a sold-out crowd. A family friend, Bill, associated with the youth team was able to pull some incredible strings and arrange for us to take behind-the-scenes tours of both Sloan and Scottsdale, given by an actual scout for the team. This was definitely a once-in-a-lifetime opportunity for the boys, who are still incredibly grateful. This included seeing the practice facilities, players' lounges, and more. The best moment though, came after we went out onto the field, where the Cubs were already deep into their practice. Our tour guide told us that they would be starting batting practice soon, and that the boys could go shag balls in the outfield! This was one of the highlights of our spring training experiences, and is the sort of thing that we are very lucky to have experienced. The boys were in heaven, sprinting for the outfield and tripping over one another while trying to get balls hit by some of the best in the business. It was a magical moment, both for the kids and the dads, as they watched from behind the dugout.

The venue is also equipped with impressive batting cages and weight rooms, which we saw as well. The boys got very excited over the buckets and buckets of gum that they certainly weren't expecting to see. The tour guide took us back to see the locker room and cafeteria, where they have water bottles and other things for the players, and we noticed many different kinds of bubblegum in huge pails. The kids went a bit nuts about the gum, and each grabbed a handful to see them through the day. MLB has been pushing that players use gum instead of smokeless tobacco products, and it seems like this trend is slowly taking off. The Giants became the first team to try and go smokeless at their stadium in 2015, so we'll see.

Like at Peoria, Sloan has an area where players can interact with fans while walking from the training facility to the field. It felt like a walk of fame! We got to walk it twice, once early on the tour heading to the stadium to watch batting practice, and then later when we left the stadium to check out the gym. The first time we made the walk there were maybe forty or fifty people milling about. The second time though, there were hundreds! There were tents set up, people grilling food, and more. The Cubs' fans must have been surprised to see us and the boys instead of the players! That was a moment that really made us feel like ballplayers, with fans three deep on either side looking our way. The boys were even asked for autographs by some of the younger kids. It was a very cool experience!

After our tour the game itself (with the Reds) was a pleasure to attend. Sloan Park is very impressive, especially when all 15,000 of its seats are filled! It was even more fun since there were so many of us... thirty-five baseball fans spread over eleven families! The atmosphere was fantastic, and the kids got caught up in it easily. The players, fans, managers, coaches, and vendors are all extremely happy to be out at the field again. A full house doesn't hurt, either!

The Cubs have some fun traditions, even during spring training exhibition games. One that we had never seen, or in this case, heard, was playing the song "Hit the Road, Jack" by Ray Charles whenever a Reds player struck out! It was a ton of fun, and the Cubs ended up winning. The Cubs also have one of the longest-serving vendors we have come across. In fact, he has become such an established figure at Cubs' spring training that he has his own baseball card! A peanuts and beer vendor for over twenty years, Mark is a real crowd pleaser, affectionately called, "Mark the Beer Guy." If you go to buy a beer from him, he whips out a very large novelty magnifying glass and inspects you, as though to investigate whether you are old enough to buy a beer!

We've mentioned that one of the most loyal fanbases belongs to the San Francisco Giants. This holds true even at spring training! The Giants play at Scottsdale Stadium, which has been around for a while, and was renovated in 2006. We had only been to this park once before our tour with the Rebels. What a great stadium! Scottsdale looks and feels new, and is one of the bigger spring training venues in the Cactus League. Couple that with very high attendance, and the exhibition games start to feel like regular season ones at places like Scottsdale and Sloan!

The game that day was at three in the afternoon, and we got there at half past nine in the morning. Even that early, there were fans waiting to see the players arrive. It was really something to see the sports cars and trucks pulling into the lot, and to see Ferraris and other sports cars revving their engines. On top of that, players like Matt Cain and Jake Peavy stepping out of them a few paces away! The crowd was anxiously guessing who was in each incredible car. It was exciting and a memory the Rebels and dads will never forget.

During the tour, we went into the stadium through the player entrance. This gave us the chance to bump into a number of players, which was very exciting. We were in the front office, getting the tour agenda, when in walked Hunter Pence, All-Star right fielder for the Giants! Pence is an amazing player, and has a unique claim...his very first MLB home run was also a grand slam! He is great with fans as well, and politely signed for the boys and chatted with them. We had just seen, about a month beforehand, a great video on ESPN where he surprised his girlfriend with a proposal at Disneyland, and Steve mentioned how fun it was to watch. It is always nice to be able to have something personal to chat with a player about!

The inner halls of the stadium, particularly in player areas, are spotted with posters and other reminders of the history of the team. They commemorate great players and moments in Giants' history, which you will remember stretches all the way back to the turn of the century in New York City.

We got to see the inside of the venue from a player's perspective, including players getting iced before the game and staff getting balls ready, and then got to see the outside in the same fashion. We were shown the home and visiting teams' dugouts before going out onto the field itself. We were warned not to touch the lines! They are easily messed up and time consuming to fix, so it is best to leave them alone and let the players be the ones to mess them up. Our tour guide that morning thought it would be exciting to have a little baseball competition on the field. He instructed the boys to race to the centerfield wall and back to the foul line in right field. It was a fun exercise for our aspiring MLB players!

After working up a sweat out in the bright Arizona sun, we went back in, to check out the Giants' clubhouse. There we were shown a cache of baseballs, and told that on average, each team orders around 700 dozen baseballs for spring training, each with a unique spring training logo on it. These are cool items for collectors, as the logo sets them apart from regular season MLB balls. One very interesting tradition we were exposed to during spring training was mud rubbing. When baseballs are new, they are smooth and a bit slick. Since almost the beginning of professional play, pitchers have rubbed various substances over the balls in order to make them rougher. The texture that resulted from rubbing the balls made them easier to grip, and easier to play with. In the 1940s, Lena Blackburne, coach with the Philadelphia A's, began looking for something that would make the balls rougher, but not stain them a darker shade, making them more difficult to see. Eventually his search led him to a riverbed location in New Jersey. The mud in this area was perfect...after rubbing a new baseball with it, the balls were left with a perfect gripping texture while remaining a nice white color. The location of this mud has been kept secret all these years, and before each spring training, major, and minor-league game, several dozen balls are rubbed in tinned mud from that same riverbed! We passed by a few equipment managers rubbing balls in the mud while on this part of the tour.

After seeing the balls we went to a lounge area, where more players were relaxing before the game by watching television or listening to music. It was a great experience for everyone, but particularly the kids on the team who might one day be players themselves! The last great touch of the tour was for the boys on the team to try on the tour guide's World

Series ring! You could see their eyes light up, as they, like every young baseball player, dream of the big leagues. This was truly a special moment.

After the tour we went into Old Town Scottsdale. Like so many cities in the Southwest, it is great for just walking and browsing. There are small galleries and museums, and plenty of great restaurants. Our attention, of course, was on the souvenir shop on Main Street! Situated next to the ever-popular Rusty Spur Saloon, Bischoff's Shades of the West was swarmed with fans, all excited about spring training. There was a real buzz of anticipation, that you only get when a bunch of eager baseball fans are gathered together in one place! Kirk alerted us to a neat twist of spring training, which is that with so many coaches, managers, umpires, and players are all condensed in a small area, the likelihood that you will run into these people out and about in the town is pretty high! This is particularly true during the evening. Since virtually all spring training games are day games, by dinner time the players and coaches are done playing for the day, and head out to local restaurants. One neat thing we recommend you do is ride on the golf carts in town...since everything is pretty close together during spring training time, it can be easy to grab a free ride on one of these to your next destination.

We went to the Oakland A's game the following afternoon, against the Cubs. This game was sold out as well, and there was a good mix of fans for both teams. Plenty of Chicago fans were in town already to see games at Sloan, so it would make sense for a lot of them to have a bit of a reunion with their old stadium. It was another beautiful day, and we got to talk with All-Star catcher, Ray Fosse. Fosse has been a broadcaster for Oakland for thirty years. He also played ball for several major league teams in the 1960s and 1970s. He is a several time All-Star, Golden Glove winner, and World Series Champion, and we were honored to have a conversation with him!

Broadcasters are a major part of the baseball watching experience, and Ray is one of our favorites. Another announcer that we love is Mark "Mud" Grant, the Padres' color commentator. Color commentators don't call games play by play, but offer up additional analysis and information to supplement the main announcer. Mark has a very engaging style, and Steve has mentioned that he will keep listening to a broadcast even if the Padres are down by many runs if "Mud" is commenting. He is famous for the various catch-phrases that he uses, the most famous of which is, "That's some kinda nice!" when something goes well for the Padres.

Back to the game! It was between the Chicago Cubs and the A's, and was a good one that got a bit scary at one point. The boys were snacking on foot-long corn dogs, when a line drive through foul territory flew right towards them! It stopped in time though, thankfully at an unoccupied seat in front of Jack. It definitely provided some chatter amongst our section, and everyone was feeling blessed that no one was harmed.

————◆————

While we have only been to that one Grapefruit League game, we definitely love southern baseball. We had a great time touring the southern states and visiting their MLB stadiums. Among the notable, Tropicana Field in Tampa Bay, where the Rays play, one of the neatest things about that park is the Rays Touch Tank! This huge tank is home to a bunch of stingless rays who spend the day swimming around past right center field, soaking in the sun and enjoying pets from the crowds. It is a like having a miniature aquarium inside a baseball stadium. The boys spent a while petting and feeding the rays up on the middle level.

The Rays were off to a slow start, and it didn't get any better the day we went to see them. They had lost the first five games of the season, and were struggling to really get going. For a little while it looked like the Rays might pull out a win, as they cut the deficit to one run behind the Angels after a home run by B. J. Upton. The Angels' Torii Hunter, All-Star, also hit a nice home run. The score was Angels 5, Rays 1, but any day spent at a ballpark is a good day! This would be the last loss in their opening streak though, and they would actually claw their way up to 91 wins, 71 losses, and a playoff spot. Just like you can never tell when a game might shoot off in an unexpected direction, so too is it impossible to tell when a team will get in the groove and turn a season around!

Sometimes being in the right place at the right time leads to interesting souvenirs. When we were at Tropicana, we made our usual trip to the gift shop and the boys ran up to Dayna and delightfully announced that they had found what they wanted...Manny Ramirez dreadlocks! Although Dayna thought that was a peculiar choice, she liked how excited the kids were when they found them, so she agreed that they could get them. You can imagine Steve's reaction when he saw two kids heading towards him with very long hair! Unbeknownst to us, that evening we saw on ESPN that Manny had gotten himself into a situation with MLB, and soon after he announced his retirement. In fact, we found out the very next morning in the paper that the wigs would no longer be sold after the game we had attended. We bought ours around 3:30, and the game was over by 3:45. Can you believe that these wigs ended up being the last ones sold in Tropicana Field? Later in that trip we took a Disney cruise that was partially Pirates of the Caribbean themed, so they came in handy there as well!

Tropicana isn't the only field in Florida that features aquatic baseball fans! There are long aquariums behind home plate at Marlins Park that feature a number of interesting tropical fish. This aquarium is less accessible than the one in Tropicana, since it is so close to the most expensive seats, but it still makes a grand impression. Don't worry, the aquarium glass is bullet-proof, so it would have no problem halting even the most blistering fastball from Aroldis Chapman!

These trends were very much on display for the game we saw at Turner Field, home of the Atlanta Braves, during our tour of the southern stadiums. The Braves, like so many other teams, can trace their history to another club in another city back in the late 1800s; in this case, the Cincinnati Red Stockings. The Braves we know and love have played out of Atlanta since 1966, and moved into Turner Field in 1997. The field was actually built for the Summer Olympics that were held in Atlanta in 1996, and after that was done, the Braves moved in.

Turner is another field that has a carnival feel to it that makes it great for people with kids. There is an area dedicated to games and interactive activities, just like Ashburn Alley, called Scouts Alley. Also check out the Skyfield atop the roof, the giant Coca-Cola bottle, and the base path for kids to run. We spent a lot of time up in that area while we watched the game and sat in the large Adirondack chairs for some additional entertainment. It is way at the top of the stands, and you can see pretty much everything. The Braves' theme includes tomahawks, and with tomahawks comes chopping! The eighth-inning Chop Rally is a fun tradition at Turner, during which a huge drum, called the Big Drum, is beaten. The Big Drum is taller than any fan, and fans get to hit it during the eighth-inning Chop as a perk for fundraising with the Braves, and during special events. It is a very unique rallying tradition!

The game started off on the slow side, with a few runs here and there until the eighth inning. Then, things went crazy! The game was 5 to 4 in Arizona's favor, and then the Braves turned on the heat after two batters were walked after being hit by the Arizona pitcher, David Hernandez. With those guys on base, Heyward, one of the Braves' outfielders, hit a double that scored a few runs and gave the home team the lead. The Braves would go on to score not one, not two, not three, but four more runs that inning, to turn a tight contest into a crushing 11 to 5 victory! Obviously we wouldn't leave a game with a 5-4 score, but the point still stands: even in the eighth or ninth inning, a team might score half a dozen runs or more out of nowhere, and you should never give up early!

There was actually a trend while we were in the south of high scoring games...no wonder the greats of a century ago wanted to head down there in the winter and spring. Maybe there is something in the air! The other big game was the Marlins against our Padres.

We flew into Ft. Lauderdale the day of the game, initially on a trip to visit the boys' grandparents. We checked into our hotel and then met up with them and headed over to the game.

Marlins Park is the newest stadium in MLB, located in Little Havana, on the site of the former Orange Bowl, where the NFL Miami Dolphins and Hurricanes played when Steve was a kid. It definitely stands out, visually, from all the others. By the time we made it to Marlins Park, we had already gone to over twenty-five different stadiums, and noticed the stark difference in style right away. Gone are the red bricks of Camden and the industrial look of the multi-use stadiums like Dodger Stadium. Everything at Marlins Park from the outside is sleek and angled, the silvery, curved exterior broken up by prominent windows. It is a very unique stadium, and time will tell if it kicks off a new trend in stadium design, the way Camden Yards did so many years ago!

Marlins Park is as contemporary inside as it is outside. It is ahead of many other parks, technologically speaking, and has actually hosted several technology conferences and events. High-speed, free Wi-Fi is offered throughout the stadium, a feature you won't find everywhere. Concessions stands have fluid displays that display food in both English and Spanish, for the large native Spanish-speaking population in the area. From a visuals and features standpoint, Marlins Park offers a different experience from many other stadiums, one that some will love and some will dislike. We thought the park was definitely a unique one to visit.

We found plenty of baseball stuff to love at Marlins Park. One thing the boys really liked was the bobblehead museum. As you well know at this point, bobbleheads are hugely popular collectibles, and are particularly valued in our family. The bobbleheads in the museum are displayed on several levels of shelving behind glass that curves as it follows the contours of the wall on the promenade level. There are hundreds of them, organized by team, from Bernie Williams to Hank Aaron to Ray Fosse. The coolest part about the whole display is that it is slightly vibrating back and forth on the platform, so all the bobbleheads are, well, bobbling their heads! It's a very funny sight, and we thought it was an inventive and cool way to display these collector's items so that they were protected, but still showing their full range.

We happened to be there during the theme night for the University of Miami. There was a great, energetic pep rally before the game out front, and the atmosphere was very exciting. Turns out it was warranted, as the home team had a great game! The Marlins took an early lead over the Padres and never gave it up. Some might have been tempted to leave, with the score sitting at 7 to 2 in the eighth inning. You might think that we were, since our team was losing. Not a chance! We ended up staying and got to see famed slugger Giancarlo Stanton, three-time All-Star and National League Home Run champion, hit a massive home run for the Marlins, the longest in the still-new stadium's history at 484 feet. That would actually end up being the second-farthest homer hit all season, and it was an amazing sight!

Spring training has been one of the most enjoyable parts of our adventure, and we're so happy we've had the opportunity to get to know the players, coaches, staff, and training facilities better during this time. We love feeling closer to our favorite teams, and it's never too early to start baseball season! We're so glad to be close enough to the Cactus League facilities to be able to get down there for fun, short trips. We're looking forward to spending more time at Grapefruit League training events in the future, because if our experience with southern baseball holds true, we'll be in for some wild games and sudden turns! We can't recommend checking out spring training highly enough to any fan!

CHAPTER EIGHT

Oh, the Places You'll Go, and the People You'll Meet

We have had many wonderful, exciting, surprising, and emotional moments at baseball games over the years. Apart from the great memories we've created during the games themselves, there is nothing in our journey that can top the fantastic people we've met and grown closer to along the way and the interesting sights we have seen. We always love meeting players, both for the first time and when reconnecting, but we also look forward to meeting coaches, grounds crew, and hospitality staff. These behind-the-scenes folks truly make the experience of attending a ballgame magical. We are constantly amazed by and grateful for their generosity and exceptional service. Many of them have gone above and beyond to help us make the most of our trips, and this book wouldn't be complete without calling attention to their incredible contributions.

Angels in the Outfield has been a Haferkamp favorite film for many years. It tells the touching story of two young baseball fans who sneak into ballgames to watch the Angels play. One of them, Roger, is a foster child, and is told by his biological father that they will be a family again when the Angels win the pennant. He means this meanly, of course, but Roger takes it to heart and prays for divine assistance on behalf of the team. Sure enough, during the next game, Roger sees angels helping the Angels make amazing plays. Eventually, the team has to win the final game on their own, and Roger and the audience learn an important lesson on dealing with loss and learning to triumph on their own.

We too have run into "Angels" and "Clubhouse Heroes" in the form of exceptional staff members, the normally invisible helpers who swoop down out of nowhere to turn an ordinary day at the ballpark into an extraordinary one. These "Angels" in the outfield include folks from the front desks and ticket counters, as well as the equipment managers who work hard and diligently prepare for each game. They are the ones who really made our trip a special one that continues to bring joy to our family, and are the unsung heroes critical to the success of every team.

One of the most dedicated stadium employees that we've met on our travels works at the Seattle Mariners' park, Safeco Field. When we first met her it was early April, and a very cold day. In fact, this game between the Rangers and Mariners was probably the coldest game we have ever been to! We had walked from our hotel, the Marriott Waterfront, and passed the Seahawks football field on our way to Safeco. We had been planning on getting tickets after snapping a few photos in front of the stadium, and had gotten there very early. There wasn't much of a line, so at the front desk we started chatting and asked her where she recommended we sit, since it was our first time at the venue. She was very enthusiastic and knowledgeable about the stadium, and personally guided us to some great seats. She also made sure the boys got their first game certificates and a pair of Safeco keychains, and offered up a lot of advice on what to do and see in the area to make the most of our trip. Thanks to her, our trip to Safeco was a great one!

In addition to hosting the coldest game we have been to, Safeco Field was also the most remote stadium on our trip. Seattle is farther north and west than any other city with a major league team, and the Northwest is a notoriously wet area. Safeco can handle rain, with its impressive retractable roof; this roof is unique throughout the major leagues, in that it doesn't seal up the entire stadium, but just offers the stands and players some moderate protection against the rain. The roof is a bit lower than other retractable roofs in the business, and is occasionally hit by fly balls. Just like at Tropicana and Wrigley, there are some special rules in place that dictate play if this happens. A ball is in play the whole time it is in flight, and either remains in play or is ruled foul based on where it lands after hitting part of the roof.

The roof wasn't hit when we were in attendance, but there was still some game-related drama. The Mariners were playing the Rangers, and the game started off with a bang, as the home team scored three runs in the first inning. Ian Kinsler of the Rangers struck back with a home run in the fourth, which brought down the mood a little. Jason Bay, outfielder for the Mariners, was also hit by two pitches, which didn't please anyone. On top of that, later in the game Kinsler tried to steal second base, and was ruled safe. A few seconds later the replay was shown up on the Jumbotron (they don't like to do this when the call is close!), and it was clear to the thousands in attendance that he wasn't safe! This was met with loud boos from the crowd; the ruling stood, though, because the Mariners hadn't challenged the call. The Mariners won in the end, 3-1, and our good luck with seeing victorious home teams held true.

Speaking of Jumbotrons, the one at Safeco Field made a lasting impression. Baseball stadiums are big places, and can fit many, many people. You might not always be able to get the best seats, and might not have the best view of the field. Some fans of the game like having detailed, thorough stats on players and teams at their fingertips, the type that baseball is famous for. Sometimes, you might just need a distraction, or something to elicit an unexpected laugh. All these needs and more are met by the wide variety of scoreboards found throughout MLB stadiums.

Scoreboards have been around since the beginning of professional baseball. They have always displayed the most important, though minimal information: the inning and the score. Over time, more detail was added, and many now display the full results of each inning, the count, and more. There is too much to check out over the course of visiting thirty stadiums, but the variety in size, location, functionality, and age of the league's scoreboards is really fascinating! Jumbotrons are definitely something that fans notice and talk about. It is very obvious, even at spring training, which ones are old. It is fascinating what they are capable of now; when the parks were just starting to digitize, some of them had low resolution and brightness. Jumbotrons are a big deal to many fans, and we recommend accounting for the view of the Jumbotron when you are looking at ticket locations and prices. There are many seats in some stadiums that offer a poor view, or no view at all, of the Jumbotron. Being able to see stats, watch instant replays in crisp detail and slow motion...these things really make attending a modern baseball game impressive. It makes a big difference to the kids particularly!

Some stadiums have held on to their old scoreboards. The two oldies, Fenway and Wrigley, both maintain and operate analog scoreboards that date from 1934 to 1937, respectively. Operators stay inside the scoreboards, and individually update the letters and numbers when they get updates on the game via computer. They are true historic treasures, and we hope they remain in use for years to come.

Many of the stadiums that we visited were built after 2000, and their scoreboards are amazing feats of engineering. Most of them double as Jumbotron screens, and offer high definition video feeds of the game from multiple angles, for the benefit of fans farther away. One of the largest such screens in use is found at Safeco Field. It is a whopping fifty-seven-feet tall and two-hundred-feet wide, and cost the team $15 million. We were a bit lucky, actually, that we got to see it in action during this trip. The screen had first been used just a week or so before, at the Mariner's opening day game. Displays like these now feature an impressive array of information: profiles of players and their batting history, scores for other games going on in the league, replays, batting order, and more. If you are attending a game for a special occasion, check and see what the prices are for getting a message displayed on the Jumbotron. When Grant got to be the Play Ball Kid years back, his name was proudly displayed on the screen!

The stats and figures appeal to die-hard fans, and the "extra" stuff appeals to everyone else. Trevor Time is an example of the creative use of these screens. We saw plenty of funny or entertaining uses on our trip. Sometimes, if there is a lull in the action, the camera will pan the crowd in Dance Mode, hoping to inspire some fan to show off their skills! Another crowd favorite activity is the Kiss Cam. Sometimes you see a quick peck, other times there is some reluctance, and sometimes it is just awkward... no matter what, the fans always get excited! Stadium managers are always coming up with inventive ways to draw the crowd together via technology, and the Jumbotron is a great example of this. The Rally Monkey is another classic. In Seattle, we got to see the much-beloved hydroplane race on the big screen. Like the presidents in D.C. and the sausages in Milwaukee, the hydroplane race is a fan favorite. The Seattle crowd displayed a level of fanaticism for this race that rivaled many of the older traditions! As the red, green, and yellow boats skip over waves, avoid the flying fish, and try to pull into the lead, it is wonderful to hear the groans and laughter from the crowd. Another one everyone seems to enjoy is the hidden baseball game, a spin on the balls and cups magic routine where a baseball is hidden under one of three hats. Many fans stop what they are doing in order to keep track of the ball as the hats shuffle around, and hopefully win the game! These scoreboards bring fans together, and give everyone something to check out and enjoy before, during, and after games. They say that everything is bigger in Texas, and when we were in Arlington, we tried taking a peek in AT&T Stadium, the home of the Dallas Cowboys, to check out their Jumbotron. At 11,520 square feet, it's one of the largest in the NFL (and larger than any in the MLB!), and by all accounts it's very impressive. We couldn't get in or get a good view on this trip, but we're eager to see it someday!

Suffice to say, Jumbotrons are a big deal! Thinking back to our trip to Safeco, the Jumbotron was definitely a highlight. It wasn't the only thing to make the trip special, however. This trip was also a little bit like Christmas for the boys when it came to getting autographs and balls from players. It was definitely cold enough to be Christmas! Safeco has an area, known as the "Pen," that is perfect for player-fan interaction, and lots of players from both teams will sign autographs there. It is located near the Mariners' bullpen out in centerfield, and features merely waist-high fencing, a dedicated kitchen led by a gourmet chef, and an unparalleled view of the field. It fills up quickly, so if you plan on staying there for the game, stake your spot early!

The boys got the Rangers' closer, Joe Nathan, to sign a ball. They were really excited about this one, as we had just seen Nathan grab his first save of the year a week earlier at the Rangers' opening day game in Arlington, Texas. They were also tossed a ball from the returning Texan catcher. A good day, but nothing compared to the next one!

Not for the first time, we were the first to get into the stadium, several hours before the opening pitch. This gave us a chance to see the sights, and watch a lot of batting and pitching practice. At the practice, the boys got balls from players on both teams, including Felix Hernandez, Mitch Moreland (Dayna is a big fan of Mitch's walk-up song, "Outsiders" by Eric Church), and more! As a matter of fact, we love walk-up songs in general. They are a great conversation starter, and you can find them listed in the MLB Ballpark app. Another one that was great back in the day was Bichette's, "Sledgehammer" by Peter Gabriel. When asked, "What would your walk up song be?" Jack quickly replied, "No One Like You" by The Scorpions. Grant proudly announced his would be "My House" by Flo Rida. Dayna's would be "Ain't that a Kick in the Head" by Dean Martin, and Steve's would be "Rapper's Delight" by the Sugar Hill Gang. A close second would be Sinatra's "Fly Me to the Moon," because it happens to be his and Dayna's wedding song! What would yours be?

Anyways, back to the game! The boys got eight balls that game, more than they knew what to do with. They both ended up giving a ball to new young fans near us who had missed out, which was a nice gesture. This kind of act, as mentioned, builds up good karma, and it is great seeing the boys help other kids get autographs. The Mariners went on to win this game as well, 4 to 3, completing a satisfying sweep in front of the home crowd.

There are countless works of art, museums, and exhibits to be found in major league stadiums, but the Baseball Museum of the Pacific Northwest at Safeco offers something a little bit unique: it is partially dedicated to teams from the area that are no longer around, like the Portland Webfeet and Seattle Rainmakers. Baseball has a long history in the area, and has seen a number of teams come and go. Along with these exhibits, the museum houses the Mariners Hall of Fame, which honors baseball greats like pitching legend Randy Johnson (thrower of the seventeenth perfect game) and beloved announcer Dave Niehaus that have been so important to Seattle baseball history. Make sure you hit this one while you're at the stadium—not only is it very interesting, but it's also a place you can get completely dry!

When we weren't watching a game, we made the most of our short time in the area by checking out the sights and sounds of Seattle. The famous Space Needle, of course, is a must-see. We had a great time at the Pike Place Market, one of the oldest farmers' markets in the country, where the boys feasted on fresh donuts, watched the famous flying fish, and put money in Rachel the Pig. The money gathered in this bronze sculpture goes to social programs associated with the Market, and we highly recommend you check her out!

At one point on the tour that first day with our Safeco "Angel," the boys had mentioned how much they wanted to come back in the future to attend one of their promotional nights, in order to get some new bobbleheads for their collection. Well, several weeks after we had gotten back home to San Diego, a package arrived. It was from her, and she had gone to several promotional nights to gather up bobbleheads, t-shirts, and several other great souvenirs for them. There is a story for us associated with bobbleheads—when Grant was very young, we had a bobblehead collection on a shelf in his room. The boys would get bobbleheads on birthdays from relatives, and we had friends and neighbors who knew what the kids liked and gave them a few. One day, the boys were running through the house and chasing after one another, and as Grant dodged into his room he suddenly and acciden-tally knocked the shelf holding his bobbleheads completely off the wall. All the bobbleheads crashed to the ground, shattering into pieces, their heads flying off all over the room. He was devastated; they were his prized possession, a collection he had built up for many years! He still to this day talks about that awful moment. According to the boys there were about fifteen bobbleheads that shattered that day; lesson learned, make sure your bobblehead shelf is taller than your growing child! Grant and this "Angel" have a special connection in that way, that she, without even knowing this story, restarted his bobblehead collection. We can't wait to get back to Safeco and see her again!

After our stint with the Mariners, we drove north and crossed the border to pay a visit to Whistler, a resort town in British Columbia about two hundred miles from Seattle. Driving hadn't been the original plan, however! Initially we had been scheduled to fly from San Diego International Airport to Vancouver International Airport. When we got to the ticket counter to check our luggage, we were asked for the boys' passports. They didn't have passports, and when we had driven across the border in the past, birth certificates had been all that was necessary. They told us that was not the case when flying, and that after September 11th, new rules were set in place. We were definitely shocked and disappointed, and thought that our trip would be ruined.

Thankfully, the airline found us a solution very quickly. The new plan was to fly into Seattle, reschedule which Mariners' games we would see, then rent a car and drive to Whistler. This ended up being a fortuitous change!

Occasionally, wildlife will make an appearance at a ball game. Squirrels and rabbits have been known to put games on hold while they prance through the well-cared for grass in the outfield, and at waterfront parks like PNC and AT&T, players can be distracted by seagulls masquerading as pop-up flies! We haven't had too many run-ins with animals in fields, but we did witness one of the strange, though necessary, lengths that grounds crew go to at Comerica Field to rid the stadium of pigeons and seagulls. When we were there in 2014, the Tigers were playing the Rays. It was the Fourth of July, and although we were expecting fireworks later, we weren't expecting firecrackers to go off in the middle of the game! Some seagulls had been congregating in foul territory, and to keep things from getting out of hand the grounds crew set off the firecrackers to scare them off. You can imagine how far we jumped out of our seats when we unexpectedly heard firecrackers going off in the middle of the game. We found out later that other methods used over the years at Comerica included black labs chasing them away, and strategically placed owl statues. We have rarely seen wildlife interfere at a baseball game, but our impromptu road trip to Whistler, where we were planning on skiing, inner-tubing, and dogsledding, made up for it. As we rounded a curve, through a clearing in the trees we spotted a full-grown black bear lumbering towards the road. We managed to snap a picture right as he glanced disinterestedly in our direction. It was the first bear the boys had ever seen, and definitely made us realize how deep we were into the mountains. If our schedule hadn't been thrown off-track earlier, we never would have seen the bear. Sometimes, things happen for a reason.

Whistler had been host to athletes during the 2010 Winter Olympic Games in Vancouver, and its slopes had seen competition in skiing, bobsledding, and more. Its location deep in the Coast Mountains was stunningly beautiful, and unlike anything the boys had seen before. There was still plenty of snow on the slopes, and we planned on enjoying some winter sports of our own.

Jack and Grant found the process of crossing the border fascinating, particularly the exchange of currencies. We did get some Canadian money during our trip, and wanted to give the boys the true tourist experience by going through the exchange process. They have kept some Canadian coins ever since as mementos, and in the hopes that we visit again soon!

Zipping around on skis in the snow was great, and we had a ton of fun on our non-baseball side-trip. Meeting the sled dogs, and the sled puppies, was great. We got to ride in a sled and take some great pictures with the puppies, and posing for pictures by the massive Olympic Rings statue. We highly recommend making a trip to Whistler, and definitely plan on going back. Whistler at any time during the year is a very interesting place, as it attracts tourists from around the world. There is always someone new to meet in the places you'll go!

Service people are great all across MLB, and we experienced exceptional service again during spring training at Hohokam Park, home of our Oakland A's. We had already had a great experience at Oakland Coliseum the day our bat was signed by so many great players. The A's had actually just moved into Hohokam after taking over the stadium from the Cubs, and we struck up a conversation with the woman at the counter. As it turned out, she had been with the team for many years, and only happened to be working the ticket desk that day. Of course, everyone on the staff was excited about the new venue and they were very eager to help guests. Eventually we told her about the journey we had completed, hitting all the stadiums, and showed her our book. She got a kick out of our story, and loved seeing pictures of us at other ballparks around the country in our family photo book. Eventually, other people showed up to grab some tickets and we went off to our seats. As we were saying goodbye to our new friend, Steve said, "Well, if you ever need a bat boy, let us know!" Out of the blue, a few days later, we got a call from this "Angel on Deck," and she told us that she had spoken to another member of the team, our "Hero in the Clubhouse," later that same day. He was more than happy to have the boys act as bat boys at spring training! Obviously being a bat boy (this is designated by "BB" on their jerseys) is a huge deal for kids, but it is a big deal for the teams as well, to know that someone reliable and presentable, who loves the game, is there to take care of the bats after a hit. It takes someone dedicated and responsible to be a bat boy, as they need to watch the game closely, and be ready to spring into action and take care of equipment. Teams value them highly and are always glad to find someone who meets these requirements!

We have since become very close with these "Angels and Clubhouse Heroes" and have remained in contact, exchanging holiday cards and so on. We truly value their friendship, and are grateful for how much they have taught us along the way! Don't just pay attention to the superstars, you never know what you might learn from other people who work behind the scenes.

Connecting with wonderful people has been a running theme throughout our spring training journeys as well. We have attended Goodyear Ballpark for spring training several times, since it is part of the Cactus League. The park is very open to the public during spring training, and we managed to meet many friendly players and employees there. One in particular tapped the boys' skills in dancing and cheering in order to get the crowd riled up, and we have several videos of them in their wigs leading the fifth inning rally call or participating in a dance-off. Grant has also been a bat boy for the Reds there, in another one of those fortunate twists. The spring training season after the year the boys had their first dance off, we were just settling into our seats when we met another "Clubhouse Hero," this one riding a golf cart. The Reds were short a bat boy, and when this happens a staff member will often zip around on a golf cart looking for a replacement. And just like that, Grant was offered volunteer work as bat boy! What started off as another case of "right place, right time" has turned into more, as now Grant is on the team's short list of bat boys during spring training and enjoys helping out each time we head to Arizona. And while it hasn't happened to the boys yet, it is only a matter of time before he falls victim to one of the teams' pranks, which is what usually happens when bat boys start getting older!

Spring training is a great time to meet the exceptional employees who keep operations ticking for the practicing teams. Grant was still excited and talking about his experience being the bat boy for then college baseball star Kris Bryant a few weeks prior when we arrived early at the Rockies spring training at Salt River Fields at Talking Stick. The Rockies were hosting the Angels, and we had all our Rockies gear on. As the usher seated us, we struck up a conversation and he complemented Grant on his crazy wig. They had a great talk about the team for a few minutes, and the usher asked him if he'd like to sit in the dugout with Troy Tulowitzki, multiple-time All Star, and the rest of the Rockies. When Grant reacted enthusiastically, the usher told him he was going to have to work for it, and told Grant he would have to be the bat boy for the Rockies in exchange! He was very excited, and had a great time with his first experience as a MLB bat boy that day!

We still go to games regularly at Petco, and have built some great relationships with the team, staff, and personnel there. One of the most rewarding relationships we have built over the years is with our friend Bud Black. Through our interactions with him, we have learned much about the kindness and loyalty that build successful teams, both on the field and off. He has put himself out on several occasions to help us on our way towards creating great memories, and we mean it when we say this book wouldn't have happened without him! There was never a game too tough for him to show anything but respect for those around him, and we never saw him brush off anyone, be they a player, member of the media, or fan.

Bud started his fifteen-season career as a pitcher with Seattle Mariners, and was a member of the 1985 World Series Championship winning Kansas City Royals. Over the course of his career, he also played for the San Francisco Giants, Cleveland Indians, and Toronto Blue Jays. He was always known as a solid left-handed starter, and began his coaching career in 2000 with Mike Scioscia of the Los Angeles Angels of Anaheim. With this team, now as pitching coach, he would win his second World Series in 2002. He became coach for the Padres in 2007, and it was in this capacity that we first started seeing him around the dugout.

One of our first memorable interactions with Bud was at spring training a few years later, and was a great example of his kindness. It was pre-game, at Salt River Field. It was one of the first times we had made an effort to get autographs on a single ball in this context, and we had gotten fourteen or so of the Padres to sign, including Bud. After the game, we were in the parking lot walking away from the park and talking about what a great day we had had, and we saw Bud again. He was dropping of a player at his car, and Steve started waving to him like they were old friends, even though they had just formally met earlier that day. Dayna was certainly surprised, and wondered who on earth Steve knew way out there in Arizona! Bud was very gracious and spent some time talking to us, and the experience was the perfect way to end the day. The kids were so excited and were talking about meeting Bud Black all the way back to the hotel from Salt River. Somehow between arriving back at the hotel and having dinner, the ball with all the signatures went missing. Whatever happened to that ball is certainly a Scooby Doo mystery! Despite the best efforts of the hotel staff who were kind enough to help us look, it was never found. We were pretty bummed, and ended up writing to Bud about it. You can imagine our surprise and delight when he sent back a wonderful, hand-written letter—along with three more signed balls!

In baseball, it has often been said that pitchers don't become great managers of players, because of their unique position in the field. Bud is one of the very few players that shatter this rule of thumb, and has built a reputation as one of the most effective communicators on the field. He manages his teams with loyalty and respect, and we were elated when he (rightfully) won Manager of the Year in 2010, one of only three former pitchers to do so.

We were surprised and disappointed when the Padres let him go in the middle of the 2015 season. The team had just rebuilt their roster, and we were looking forward to seeing how Bud would shape the new players. The dismissal shocked a lot of players and fans, as he is one of the sport's most respected and tenured managers. We're looking forward to seeing him in his new role as a special assistant to Billy Eppler for the Los Angeles Angels, and we'll be sure to continue following him as he goes forward in his career!

One of the coolest things we noticed about Bud was how he always made time to acknowledge the contributions of every member of the stadium team. Two hours before every game at Petco Park, all the ushers get together to yell out, "Go Padres!" Bud would always interrupt whatever he was doing to wave and acknowledge them. He knew that showing respect and appreciation for the workers was important, and that they were all a part of his team. During his tenure at Petco, he always took the time to chat with the boys, and pose for a picture or two. He is just fantastic at connecting people together; under Bud's influence, everyone was a valued member of the team, not just the players—the staff and the fans as well. The boys will always cherish the time they spent with Bud down by the Padres dugout. He shared a lot of great energy and positivity with us all, and really helped welcome everyone into the Padres family.

Bud Black and the Louisville Slugger Museum are definitely near the top of our lists for favorite baseball people and places, but there were several places we loved that weren't baseball related as well. Two of our favorite stops along the way were the Rock and Roll Hall of Fame and the Pro Football Hall of Fame. We incorporated these sites into our trip to the Cleveland Indians' park, Progressive Field, in 2010. From a baseball perspective, this ended up being one of the most action-packed legs of our entire trip!

The attitude in the city was contentious when we arrived. Cleveland takes its sports very seriously, and there had been some drama brewing for several months. LeBron James, one of the greatest basketball players in history, had played the first seven years of his professional career with the Cleveland Cavaliers, starting in 2003. He had become the darling of the city, and brought the Cavaliers out of a slump of losing records to several playoff appearances.

At the end of the 2006 season, he signed a new contract with the Cavaliers, which gave him the option, at the end of three years, to assume free agency and seek out a new team. Well, just two weeks before we got to the city, he announced (to the surprise of both fans and team management) that he would be exercising this option and leaving to play for the Miami Heat. When we got to the baseball game, there were people out front with placards that said, "The Good, the Bad, the Ugly, and the Quitter!" The "good" were the Indians; even though they had a losing record at the time, the home crowd was loyal and would never give up on them! The "bad" were the Boston Red Sox, with whom the Indians have had a long and bitter rivalry. The "ugly" was A-Rod (Alex Rodriguez, called "A-roid" by the fans) and the "quitter" was James. We are sure all is forgiven now that James is back!

A-Rod has had an up-and-down career, as any baseball fan will know. He has won the World Series, been named to the All-Star team, and won MVP, Golden Glove, and other awards. The reason he was so poorly received on the protestors' signs was that, a year before, he had admitted to using performance enhancing drugs in the early 2000s. He would eventually be suspended for over two hundred games as a consequence of his actions during that time, but was still active back in 2010. He was playing with the visiting Yankees, and the local fans were pretty disdainful. The fans were particularly vocal then because A-Rod had just hit his 599th career home run four days before. This meant he was looking to become only the eighth player to hit over six hundred home runs on their home turf.

Amidst all this drama, we arrived at Progressive Field. We had a great time, right from the beginning. After checking out the protestors, we ventured over to a section of a side street that had been blocked off to give kids an area for baseball activities. There were pitching, throwing, and hitting stations, as well as a mini whiffle ball field. Jack and Grant loved it, and by the time we got to our seats, they were pumped up and ready for the game.

Progressive Field has been a guest favorite for many years, and visiting this award-winning stadium is a must for any baseball fan. Four hundred fifty-five straight games were sold out from 1995 to 2001, a true testament to the park's lasting popularity and ability to draw people in for games at all points during the season. A few years before our visit, construction ended on the beautiful Heritage Park, a memorial situated past centerfield that honors past greats in Indians history. Heritage Park features a ring of impressive obelisks bearing the names of Bob Feller, Mike Hargrove, and other members of the Cleveland Indians Hall of Fame.

Even though many of the Indians fans booed A-Rod when he stepped onto the field, the historic possibility had brought in plenty of spectators, and the park was nearly sold out. The stadium was abuzz with anticipation, as fans congregated in the outfield hoping to snag an historic ball.

It was not to be, sadly! The Yankees did coast to a 3 to 2 victory over the disappointed Indians, but it would take A-Rod another week and a half to hit his six hundredth home run. It's a shame we missed it, but we loved our visit and can't wait to head back to Progressive.

Baseball may be our main sport, but we are big football fans as well, and we had to make a stop at the Pro Football Hall of Fame in Canton, Ohio.

For the most part, we were decked out in Pittsburgh Steelers gear for the occasion, but it isn't easy to separate Grant from his Pirates hat! The Hall of Fame is a great place, a window into the past of another great game. The Hall has a full-sized football field on the grounds that was perfect for running a play or two with other museum-goers, and footballs are available for this very thing. All told, it was a very educational and entertaining experience for the whole family. As it happens, there is something of interest even for the most dedicated baseball fan at the Football Hall of Fame. Deion Sanders, football legend, was inducted into the Hall in 2011. What many don't realize is that he had a stint in major league baseball as well. He played in over six hundred professional baseball games, and is the only person to ever play in both a Super Bowl and World Series! If you plan on going, consider heading out in the first two weeks in August, when new players are enshrined into the annals of football history. The whole place is impressive and high-tech.

The Rock and Roll Hall of Fame is only about an hour drive north from the Pro Football Hall of Fame, so a quick visit was called for. It was a huge change of pace, and it was nice to get out of the sports mindset and enjoy something different as a family. There is always at least some connection, though—there are many songs that have become classics at baseball games that were written by Hall of Fame inductees. Neil Diamond's "Sweet Caroline," is sung at Red Sox games, and Billy Joel's "Piano Man," is played by the Mets at Citi Field during the top of the eighth. The boys' favorite exhibit was probably the huge, glittering guitar displayed in honor of Michael Jackson.

We have picked up some networking and courtesy tips over the years that we hope will be of use to our readers. Of course, many of them you will be familiar with already, and the main tip here is the same as when dealing with players: be polite! We have been the recipients of so many kindnesses, both large and small, and always do our best to get a hand-written thank-you note to anyone who took the time to help us. Sometimes these notes contain family pictures as well, or in the case of an autograph-signing player, a picture of the player with the boys. We also ask them to sign our family book when possible, to make them feel like the superstars they are!

Along the way you will start running into a lot of people who look familiar in the stands themselves. The first summer, for example, you might run into someone that you had first met across the country a few weeks before. Over the years, we realized that other fans were doing something similar to our own journey, and it was always great to stumble across another family and touch bases. How many stadiums had they visited? Any interesting games? Had they seen that grand slam, or walk-off? And so it goes!

People will start to get engaged in the journey alongside you. One time, we ended up meeting a dad from Alabama with his three boys on the subway en route to a Chicago White Sox game. It turned out that they were also on a quest to "hit 'em all." We have kept in touch, and got together for a game at Petco when they came for the first time to strike it off their list. They are almost done with their tour, and it has been a lot of fun getting to know them! Traveling to games via public transportation will give you these kinds of opportunities, so keep an eye out for fellow fans when taking the subway, shuttle, or bus, and strike up a conversation!

The only thing baseball fans like to do more than watch the game is talk about it. Baseball is a thinker's game, slower than many professional sports, so there is a lot of downtime for fans to chat about plays. We have spoken about this with our friend Kirk quite a bit. Every single pitch has its own set of unique variables that make it different than the play before and the play that will come after. The elements at play are often staggering, and we don't envy coaches and managers who have to balance batting orders, the count, switch hitters, pinch hitters, designated hitters, bunting, balks, and steals all at once! One of the great thinkers of the game is Billy Beane. Beane played as a major league outfielder for many years, and would later become general manager and vice president for the Oakland Athletics. His time as general manager for the A's was the inspiration for the book *Moneyball* by Michael Lewis, which would later be turned into one of our favorite movies. We were honored to meet him at Hohokam during spring training, and can vouch for the fact that he is not only a brilliant general manager with incredible knowledge of the game, but an extremely friendly guy as well!

Every game you go to will have a least a few unique elements, and with the wealth of information online, it is easy to improve your knowledge of the game and dive right into the complications! Don't be afraid to talk to fellow fans on the concourse, at the outfield fences, or while waiting in line for concessions. You never know what the person next to you might know, and due to the complexity of the game, you will never run out of things to talk about! Just ask folks where they're from and who they root for to break the ice. You never know what you may find out, or the relationships you might form!

Learning more about baseball is going to enhance your experience in every way, and begins at home! Like any other interest, hobby, or passion, professional baseball has its own terminology and a fascinating history that the fans are very proud of. Be sure you're ready to strike up great conversations at the stadiums by checking out some of the many great books and movies about baseball.

Many of our family favorites are educational books about the history of the sport, the stadiums, teams, and players. There are so many wonderful stories to tell, and so many great books that tell them. Here are some of our favorites:

- *H is for Homerun: A Baseball Alphabet,* written by Brad Herzog and illustrated by Melanie Rose. We read this one over and over!

- *The Berenstain Bears Play T-Ball,* by Stan and Jan Berenstain.

- *Take Me out to the Ballpark: An Illustrated Tour of Baseball Parks Past and Present* by Josh Leventhal. The boys loved this book, because it was ballpark by ballpark, and they used it as a tool to help them choose which stadium they wanted to go to next. Every night at bedtime we would read about a different stadium. They wanted to know all the facts about how many people it would hold, when it was built, any name changes of stadium, records, and milestones at each park and so on.

- *Roberto Clemente: Pride of Pittsburgh Pirates* by Jonah Winter, illustrated by Raul Colon.

- *My Baseball Book* by Gail Gibbons.

- *Who was Jackie Robinson?* by Gail Herman, illustrated by John O'Brien.

- *Who was Babe Ruth?* by Joan Holub, illustrated by Ted Hammond.

- *The Contract* and *Hit and Miss* by Derek Jeter.

- *Where Nobody Knows Your Name: Life in the Minor Leagues of Baseball* by John Feinstein. The other books in this list are mostly geared towards kids. This is a more adult book, and is a great supplement to the books listed in the bibliography.

And here are some movies!

- *Sandlot* (entire series) (1993, PG)

- *The Rookie* (2002, G)

- *Money Ball* (2011, PG-13)

- *Everyone's Hero* (2006, G)

- *Field of Dreams* (1989, PG)

- *Angels in the Outfield* (1994, PG)

- *Trouble with the Curve* (2012, PG 13)

- *The Million Dollar Arm* (2014, PG)

- *AirBud, Seventh Inning Stretch* (2002, G)

- *Chasing 3000* (2008, PG)

Sporting events of all kinds offer a great way to meet new people, but they also offer the chance to strengthen bonds that already exist between friends, family, co-workers, or other groups. Since baseball games offer something for all age groups, and at every price point, they can be an ideal way to get new employees to get to know one another. We wanted primarily to share these experiences as a family, but even those without kids can utilize the opportunities a stadium provides. It is easy to bond as a group when cheering for a home team!

Ballgames are an experience, and part of this experience revolves around the food. In-park food stations, and the people who run them, are an intrinsic part of what gives a stadium its character. Many stadiums take pride in their local food. Several retired baseball players are associated with food stops inside major league stadiums. This is how we met Manny Sanguillén, for example, who signs autographs at Manny's BBQ at PNC before nearly every game. Another nice stop is Boog's Barbeque at Camden Yards. "Boog" Powell, a former Oriole himself, can often be found working behind the scenes at the food stand in the stadium. Food is a great way to bond with your group and meet new people. Even if you haven't yet made it to all of the stadiums, but have a hankering for some cuisine that is highly localized and rare outside of specific ballparks, Nationals Park's "Taste of the Majors" stop has you covered. They offer tasty treats from stadiums all over North America, and offer a constantly rotating menu that features everything from pierogies to Cuban sandwiches.

We started going to baseball games as a family before smart phones were the ubiquitous, powerful tools they are today. Social media offers a number of ways to support your team, find out about special events, and get more out of your ballpark experience. "Like" your favorite team on Facebook, and follow them on Twitter. Even mascots have their own pages! Teams are increasingly promoting special events and deals exclusively through these platforms, so if you are planning on attending a lot of games it might be worth checking them out regularly. They can also be a way to kick start conversations at concession stands, maintain contact with amazing people you meet along the way, or publicly thank outstanding service people. Sometimes social media can be a source of unexpected entertainment, like when the Toronto and Kansas City public libraries took to Twitter in 2015 to bicker and taunt one another over whose baseball team would win the American League Championship Series!

One of the benefits of seeing more than one game per trip when first visiting a stadium is that you can spread out your activities, and see interesting attractions elsewhere in the stadium. Many stadiums have an area designed for kids that can be a great place to meet other baseball families. The Coke bottle slide area at AT&T Park is a great one! There is also Bernie's slide in Milwaukee, and the close-by miniature model of the stadium. The model includes a miniature version of the slide! The area is a great spot to unwind between innings and interact with other parents and kids.

Beer and baseball have gone together for a long, long time. In the 1870s and 1880s, beer was introduced as a game beverage when an early rival to the National League, the American Association, started to allow sale of alcohol at its games. The National League thought poorly of this move, and the American Association was disdainfully called the "Beer and Whiskey League" for several years. The American Association ended up being on the side of history, however, as other major and minor leagues adopted the practice after its popularity was proven.

While cheap beer has been standard fare at MLB parks since the end of prohibition, many stadiums in recent years have started offering more distinguished selections. Several Wisconsin brewing companies offer their high-quality beverages at Miller Park in Milwaukee. AT&T Park, Petco Park, and Safeco Field in particular offer an incredibly wide selection of beer from local and national breweries. Steve had a great time trying out new brews while on our trip, and these concession booths can be the perfect place to network with other baseball and beer fans. One of his favorites is The Craft Pier by Ballast Point, located in right field at Petco. Ballast Point is a well-established, local brewery that offers a great selection of crafted beer. Steve's personal favorite is their Pale Ale...the perfect thing for a hot San Diego day at the ballpark!

A more cost-effective, novel option that we came across was the nifty self-serve beer machines at Target Field that were in use during the All-Star Game in 2014. They had a pretty limited selection, but were a ton of fun to use, and broke the ice all by themselves when it came to getting to know those in line! Any way you get it served, it never hurts to offer a beer to a new friend in the ballpark who has given you a great tip or offered you some fantastic advice!

We have one more tip for you before heading into the final leg of our journey! Several times in our book we stress the importance of staying late at baseball games. We definitely learned this one the hard way! There were a few instances where we cut it a bit close when it came to leaving one stadium to head to another. After seeing the Blue Jays play in Toronto in early July, 2012, we hopped in the car right away and drove for six hours straight. We got to PNC in Pittsburgh during the third inning of the Pirates' game against the Astros. We were late partially because we had gone to check in at our usual hotel beforehand, the Springhill Suites across from the stadium. The plan was to catch the game going on, go back to the hotel and sleep, then meet up with Dayna's family for the game and fireworks the next day, the 4th of July.

The game was a close one, and we were all pretty tired, especially the boys. We also were a bit far from the action, as we had rushed from the ticket counter and could only get basic tickets. The Pirates were losing by three runs when we got to our seats. They had managed to claw back and tie the game up in the fourth, after a rally started by a McCutchen home run. By the seventh inning the Pirates were winning, and we thought the game was almost over. Then, the Astros tied it up again in the ninth! We were absolutely exhausted, and even though it had been a great game, Steve caved to the boys' wishes and we stumbled out of the stadium and started to walk to the hotel. After all, it was looking like extra innings anyways. But just then, as we were crossing the street, we heard a massive roar from the home crowd. We dashed up the stairs to our room and flipped on ESPN, to find that Drew Sutton had hit a towering home run with one out tallied, giving the Pirates a walk-off victory! You can bet we were kicking ourselves for leaving when we did. Lesson learned...now we stay until the bitter end!

CHAPTER NINE

Grand Slam

A grand slam is a home run hit with bases loaded, and is one of the ultimate plays in baseball. It is something every player and fan dreams of accomplishing or seeing, and very few things approach the excitement of a game-ending grand slam! The *Field of Dreams* side trip was a great way to head into the final "grand slam" stop on our trip: the All-Star Game at Target Field in Minneapolis, on July 15, 2014. We had known for some time that the game would be at Target Field, and since we wanted to end our tour of all of the major league baseball stadiums with a bang, we had decided to wait until the All-Star Game to visit. We had gotten to the point in planning for our journey where only four stadiums remained: Comerica Park (home of the Tigers) in Detroit, Busch Stadium (home of the Cardinals) in St. Louis, Kauffman Stadium (home of the Royals) in Kansas City, and Target Field (home of the Twins) in Minneapolis. We decided to hit them all in one big eleven-day trip. While we were always excited for each of the games and stadiums we experienced, it couldn't really get better than heading from the Field of Dreams to the All Star game!

Comerica Park, built in 2000, rides the fence between the retro, red brick look of the stadiums inspired by Camden and the more modern stadiums like Marlins Park that stray into modernist territory. The entrance into the park is very cool. The archway is flanked on both sides by two massive baseball bats, each eighty feet tall. Above and to the side of these, several stone tiger sculptures stalk the stadium, looking down at the lines of fans coming to watch the game, no doubt hungry for visiting fans. There is also a gigantic tiger statue that you can take pictures with.

Jack and Grant could easily have both fit inside its mouth! More tigers can be found throughout the park, from the top of the scoreboard to the merry-go-round.

We were there to see the Tigers and Rays play. The boys had a great time getting autographs before the game, the main prize being a signature from the Ray's relief pitcher Grant Balfour. Our seats were great, right on the line near the linesmen. This is a great place to get a ball or two from the linesmen, and we recommend sitting there if you get the chance! It was a rollercoaster of a game, and tightly fought. It was tarnished a little bit by some batters being hit by pitchers, which led to heated tempers that in turn led to the ejection of the then Rays' manager, Joe Madden, three-time Manager of the Year and World Series champion. These things happen, but they are very rare! Baseball is a passionate game sometimes. We enjoyed the game, and saw a few great hits, including a home run from the visiting team's third baseman, Evan Longoria.

We had flown in that day, gone right to the hotel to check in, and then walked to the stadium. We didn't spend too much time in Detroit, unfortunately, but we can vouch for the quality of the Comerica Park, and the quality of the food at the Hockeytown Café! This is a reference, of course, to Detroit's reputation for undying loyalty to their many-time Stanley Cup winning Detroit Red Wings. From there we continued on to St. Louis, as we mentioned way back in chapter three.

One of the last games we saw before the All-Star Game was a wild one! We were in Kauffman Stadium for a game between the Tigers and Kansas City Royals. Historically, it was a battle between one of the oldest franchises and one of the newest; while the Tigers have a baseball tradition stretching back to the 1890s, the Royals are one of the teams that was founded during MLB expansion in the 1960s. The Royals have played at Kauffman for almost their entire history, their only other stadium having been the Kansas City Municipal Stadium from 1969 to 1972.

One of the most prominent features of Kauffman Stadium is the amazing system of fountains behind centerfield, celebrating Kansas City's designation as the City of Fountains (it has more fountains than any other city in the world except Rome, Italy!). The stadium boasts one of the largest examples of these types of fountains in the world, and it is lit from underneath by multi-colored lights. The system is over three-hundred feet long, and runs through most of the game, putting on a special show if the home team hits a home run or wins a game. A few years ago, the fountains would often jet water over a hundred feet in the air, but some recent seat additions have cut that back a bit! It is possible to watch the game from above and behind the fountains, from a concourse that also features several statues that honor past Royals.

We loved the Royals' unique Jumbotron! It is one of the largest and most impressive in MLB, and was actually the largest color display in the world for several years. It is right in the middle of the outfield, and gives a great view to nearly the entire audience. It also has some unusual dimensions; it is taller than it is wide, and comes to a tapered point at the bottom. Its tall shape makes it great for displaying full profiles of players. Finally, it is topped with a truly royal crown!

We had very good seats, with a wonderful view of the full moon and fountains for the night game. The seats were GordoNation seats, in a fan area dedicated to cheering Alex Gordon. They came with t-shirts, which we thought was terrific! We actually have a dear friend named Gordon, so they made a great surprise present for him! We had gotten there early, when it was still light out, so that the boys could spend some time at the Outfield Experience, one of the largest kids' zones in any stadium we have been to. They seemed to have everything; a stage for live music and shows, mini-golf, playgrounds and carnival rides, and the much-loved pitching, batting, and running practice stations. Equipped with concessions as well, it could very easily be a place to stay for the entire game! Steve enjoyed some of Kansas City's finest BBQ at Sweet Baby Rays, while Dayna and the boys enjoyed Topsy's famous popcorn. Both had long lines but were well worth the wait!

The game was a big one. At the time, the Tigers and Royals were first and second in the AL Central division, respectively, and were starting a four-game series in Kansas City. The stakes weren't through the roof, but they were high enough to give the game some extra spice. The Tigers got off to a fast start, scoring three runs in the first inning. The Royals struck back in the second inning, only to be scored on three more times in the fourth. The Royals notched another run after Billy Butler hit a nice home run. Unfortunately for the Royals, that four-run difference was as close as they would get, as the Tigers would surge ahead and score a crazy eight more runs in the fifth inning. The final score would be 16 to 4. It was a sad day for the home team, but a great day of baseball for fans that enjoy watching every team. It was actually one of the highest-scoring games we saw outside of spring training. The trip wouldn't be complete without a neat souvenir, and this time the boys settled on a gigantic, oversized baseball. The plan was to take it to Fan Fest for autographs; it was quite humorous seeing the expressions on players' faces when they were asked to sign it! It has definitely been a conversation starter.

After this game we made our road trip up to Minneapolis. We didn't dive into the All-Star game right away, however. We had planned ahead and arrived in time to attend all the events that surround it, including Fan Fest and the Home Run Derby. Once arriving in Minneapolis, we checked into the Courtyard by Marriott downtown and went down to Fan Fest.

Fan Fest was held at the Minneapolis Convention Center, and had more to check out than we would ever be able to get through. It actually ran from the 11th to the 15th, and we had gotten there early so that we could spend at least one full day going up and down the aisles, looking at all the great stuff on display. It was a treasure trove of baseball knowledge and gear. There were collectors' booths where it was possible to buy, sell, or trade all manner of baseball souvenirs and memorabilia, including cards, signed bats and balls, and baseball pins.

The baseball pin collections were particularly eye-opening for us—in all our travels, we had never heard of them! We have since begun our own collection of pins. Because they are easy to make, there are pins for everything from major league teams to local softball teams, and everyone in between. There were a few collectors nice enough to give the boys a quick introduction to the hobby and the history of certain pins, and from then on, Jack and Grant were committed to finding as many rare pins as possible! We definitely wish we were aware of them sooner. They are small, easily carried around and stored, and complement a card and ball collection nicely. Well, we have at least one excuse now to re-visit every park!

There were also Q&A sessions with both active and retired players, managers, and more. For autograph hunters, Fan Fest is paradise. The boys came out with plenty of newly signed items for their collection, having been lucky enough to meet David Winfield, Rollie Fingers, and Fergie Jenkins, among others. It does take work though. Be prepared! If you want autographs, follow our habits laid out in our third chapter: bring multiple pens, keep extra balls in your pockets, and so on. Be polite, and patient, and persistent. Autograph signings are more structured at Fan Fest, and you will have to be prepared to wait in lines from time to time. Make sure you know what the signing schedules are and as usual, arrive early.

There are a lot of Hall of Famers at the autograph signings. There is also a representative from MLB who authenticates the items right after they are signed. He stamps them with a holographic stamp that identifies them as authentic autographs. Once your turn comes, you get your signature, then move down to the next station for authentication: it is a very well-oiled system! There are important non-players as well. We were honored to meet Roberto Clemente's wife, Vera, for example. Clemente is such an icon for Pittsburgh baseball; it was exciting to get to meet her, and we had a wonderful conversation.

It's really important to get the schedule of the Fest and set a plan for the day, otherwise the lines and crowds could be overwhelming. There is so much to do! You really have to prioritize what you want to see. It is very easy to miss out on an autograph you might want if you don't get to the line soon enough. We got in line very early to meet Dave Winfield, for example. As we have recommended earlier, ask the folks you are meeting with a question, as a way to get a conversation going. For example, we asked Dave Winfield what advice he would give to the boys as young players. He happily replied, "Enjoy the game, especially as a youth, and have fun!"

Also, check ahead of time and see if you can have the players sign an object you choose yourself. We ran into a few autograph booths where players had endorsement deals with different companies, and the only thing the players would sign were branded photographs. Obviously these still make fantastic items for your collection, and some people prefer a signed photograph because the maintenance is easier than a ball. Fan Fest is much more manageable a few days before the All-Star Game and Home Run Derby get started, so we highly recommend coming out as soon as the doors open. These two events draw very large crowds, and there will be a lot of competition in autograph lines.

Fan Fest is a great place for baseball fans of all ages. Jack and Grant had a wonderful time meeting all the mascots who were there representing their teams' spirit, and even had a happy reunion with the Padres' Friar, who, like us, had made it all the way from San Diego—though maybe not by way of Kansas City! All, or nearly all, of the team mascots are at Fan Fest, so this is a great time to meet the ones you may have missed on other days, and a cool opportunity to get them to all sign their own autographs on a memento of your choosing. There were also life-sized cutouts of players so that you could take photos with those who weren't in attendance, and some incredible collections of memorabilia.

There are a lot of extra activities sponsored by various companies. Hitting and pitching stations, and performance drills, and even a station where you can be an announcer! The boys' favorite station was the base running one, because they beat the virtual MLB player every time. There are also countless photo opportunities...not only with the live players, coaches, staff, mascots, and cardboard cut-outs, but also stations where you can try on jerseys and pretend to be a player, fancy sponsored cars to sit in, gigantic baseballs, and more. In short, it is a feast of baseball fun and lore. Don't go for just an hour or two. The convention is only once a year, and you really should make the most of it and spend at least a day, if your schedule allows it!

Target Field is one of the more modern stadiums in major league baseball, construction having finished in 2009. The Minnesota Twins, interestingly enough, are one of the oldest franchises in the league, having been initially formed as the Washington Senators in 1901 as one of the founding eight teams in the National League. Since moving to Minnesota in 1960, the Twins have called six different parks home, Target Field being the latest and greatest.

And great it is! Target Field is one of the premier parks in North America, and offers an impressive array of features and amenities. The stadium is on the smaller side and seats just over 40,000 fans. Its main structure is fairly unique, as it is made out of locally sourced golden limestone that gives its facades a striking appearance. There are several full-sized restaurants in the stadium, one of which is dedicated to season ticket holders. Steve particularly liked the self-serve beer stations, which were introduced during the All Star festivities.

Anyone with even the slightest interest in art will find plenty to love at Target Field. The main entrance to the park is nicely landscaped, and is punctuated by a series of statues, the largest of which is a 1,500-pound bronze glove! There is also a memorial wall erected in homage to past players. Periodically, fans are able to purchase their own memorial spots on the wall, which is a combination of etched stone and glass, and take their place right alongside the players as an integral piece of Twins' history.

One thing the designers had in mind might seem fairly obvious to spectators, but isn't well addressed at some stadiums: the view of the game! There are both apps and websites that you can use to see what your view would be like from a certain seat, so you can be prepared before actually purchasing tickets. Virtually every seat in Target Field has a fantastic view of the playing field, from behind home plate to the private suites to the nosebleeds, where we happened to sit. Like Nationals Park, Target Field features a wide open concourse, so that wherever you are, be it waiting in line for food or running to the bathrooms, you can see through the structure to the field.

After spending a lot of time, and some money, at Fan Fest, we were ready for the Home Run Derby. The Home Run Derby rules have evolved over the years, with some controversy. Simply put, it is a competition to see which player can hit the most home runs. Over the course of several rounds, these accomplished hitters take big swings at easy throws lobbed by pitchers from behind wire barricades, in an attempt to hit as many as possible over the fence.

The Home Run Derby is a huge hit with the kids, being able to see home run after home run. It is pure anticipation and excitement. There are few events in any sport as iconic as a home run, and the Derby is dedicated to them! Part of what makes the Home Run Derby so exciting is not knowing what to expect. Since the rules have changed over the years, you never know how many home runs you are going to see, or what the pace will be. There might be only a handful in a given round, or you might see Josh Hamilton belt out twenty-eight in a single round, like he did in 2008! To make things even more exciting, there are special little twists from year to year. For a number of years, there have been golden balls and flex balls; if a player hit one of these over the fence for a home run, MLB and participating companies would make donations to charity based on the previous number of home runs hit that round. The crowd certainly gets excited when one of these is up for hitting!

Earlier in the book, we explained the difference between a hitters' field and a pitchers' field. Well, Target Field has a bit of a mixed reputation in this regard, but one thing is certain; with its twenty-three-foot wall in right field, left-handed hitters didn't have an easy time of hitting homers during the regular season. It might come as no surprise that the only lefty in the group of ten at the derby only hit two.

The event started out during a light drizzle that eventually cleared up, but not before gracing the gathered fans and players with a phenomenal rainbow. The opening pitch was pretty interesting, as four great Minnesota players all threw at the same time! The boys were very excited once the rain stopped. They, along with Aunt DeeDee and Uncle Joel, enjoyed hot chocolate sold by strolling vendors, as it was a chilly night and All-Star-themed blankets were selling out fast. It was their first derby, and they were ready for it to get started! Home run derbies are individual rather than team competitions, so Jack and Grant's allegiances quickly gravitated towards players that they had acquired autographs from or met. This strategy would eventually pay off!

First up was Todd Frazier of the Cincinnati Reds, a great player that we have seen several times before, who was participating in his first Derby. He was pitched to by his brother, Charlie, who had been drafted by the Marlins in 1999, and now owns his own baseball academy for kids. It was touching to watch! Todd came in second, but he would meet with great success the following year, winning the Derby in front of a home crowd back at the Great American Ballpark. This was the first time in twenty-five years that a player had won the derby in front of a home crowd, since Ryne Sandberg had done it in 1990. The boys were lucky enough to talk with Sandberg, a Hall of Famer, during our behind-the-scenes tour at Sloan. Giancarlo Stanton, whom we had seen homer during a regular game, was a definite crowd favorite, hitting several staggering home runs over the center field fence and up into the third level of seating. He even got a standing ovation from the other fans after his last five hundred footer. The boys were satisfied with the winner in 2014, Yoenis Céspedes. He was playing for the Athletics at the time, and the boys had managed to get his autograph before at spring training. He was on fire, and hit significantly more home runs than the other guys. It was definitely his moment to shine, and we are glad he won! Hopefully in the future, the boys will get to play in the outfield at the Home Run Derby, scrambling after balls that fall just short of the fence. It's nice to dream, in baseball anything can happen!

The All-Star Game is always a big affair. It features AL players on one team, and NL players on the other, so people come from all over to watch their stars. The current selection process is as follows: fans get to vote online for the starting fielders, and managers vote to select the pitchers. Reserves are selected partly by managers, and partly by the players themselves. While the atmosphere is more relaxed and fun than most other games, the players are still competitive professionals, and make sure to put on a good show.

After an impressive and patriotic flyby from six USAF Thunderbirds, the game got underway. It was something of an historic game, as it was the last All Star game Derek Jeter, legendary New York Yankee, would ever play. He had announced earlier in the year that he would be retiring after the close of the 2014 season, and so his fourteenth All Star appearance was a special one. He certainly made the most of this game, starting off with an incredible diving snag of a fierce grounder hit by McCutchen. He didn't quite get the out, but the audible gasp in shock at the play from the stands was amazing. Even McCutchen shook his head in amazement at the energy and drive of the legendary Yankee.

Jeter was given the honor of batting first for the NL team, and his introduction to the plate was met with a standing ovation from the fans. We got chills listening to the deep chant from the crowd..."Derek Jeter, Derek Jeter!" It lasted for some time, and members of the opposing team even took off their gloves to join in. After passing on the first pitch, he hit a practiced drive deep into right field and reached second with ease, to the roar of the crowd. On the very next pitch, his teammate Trout hit a triple, and Jeter scored a run. His second at-bat saw another hit to right field, this time on a full count, and he finished the game batting 1.000.

The rest of the game featured a little bit of everything, as everyone hopes an All-Star game will. Miguel Cabrera hit a nice home run in the first inning over the left field wall on the way to a 3 to 0 lead for the AL. NL players would respond with back-to-back doubles, and reduce that lead to 3 to 2. Derek Jeter received another standing ovation in the fourth inning when he was relieved, longer and louder than the rest of the players. Although the NL would make the game a tie, the final score was in favor of the AL, 5 to 3. The players wear their actual team jerseys, so it is very neat to look out onto the field and see a bunch of players from different teams, working together to play a great game.

There are several really cool traditions that have sprung up in recent years around the All-Star game. One of our favorites involves the statues! Since the early 2000s, cities hosting the All-Star game, in conjunction with MLB, have put together collections of large, thematic statues to give the event a special flair. There were a few years when there weren't any statues, but most host stadiums have had their own neat edition. We had actually seen quite a few of these statues before even getting to Target Field, as they sometimes become permanent installations. They are usually brightly colored, and commemorate aspects of the host city's history, generally with a different one for each team. We saw some Mickey Mouse statues in Anaheim (home to Disney), for example, and the Royals-themed Statue of Liberty in Kansas City. This one had actually come from New York, where the 2008 All-Star game was held. There were a total of forty-two statues that year, scattered around the city: thirty that were themed for each team in MLB, and others to honor old teams (like the Brooklyn Dodgers) and leagues. When the All-Star game was actually held in Kansas City, the statues were huge baseballs, also themed for various teams, resting inside of "royal" crowns. From mustaches in Cincinnati to cactuses in Phoenix, the statues are always a great attraction!

The year we went to Minneapolis, the statue theme was the Peanuts, in honor of the famous cartoon penned by Minneapolis-born Charles Schulz. They were baseball themed, of course, with several of the famous crew wearing Twins jerseys. Snoopy himself was leaning against a giant baseball that featured the logos of all the major league teams. They added a nice touch to the celebrations, and offered even more photo opportunities. Collectors should note that the themed statues each year are also available during Fan Fest as limited-edition smaller statues and pins. For the truly adventurous, sometimes the full-sized statues are put up for auction afterwards—imagine having that in your yard!

The All-Star Game, or "Midsummer Classic," is one of baseball's most revered traditions, and dates back to 1933. On our tour of Chicago, we had been able to see the stunning architecture that graces the city's skyline. In 1933, this beautiful city was host to the Chicago World Fair, a successor in spirit to the Columbian Exhibition of 1893. As part of the fair, a baseball game was organized. As this was meant to be an exhibition game worthy of the setting, some of the best players of the day, from many different teams, were invited to participate. A few of these players you might recognize...Babe Ruth and Lou Gehrig come to mind! The MVP award for the All-Star game was, for a time, named the "Arch Ward Trophy," in honor of the sports editor for the *Chicago Tribune* who was so instrumental in getting the first All-Star game off the ground so many years ago. Mike Trout was the winner when we attended, joining a long line of storied players!

This was one game where we didn't really try to get autographs. It's a lot tougher to get into autograph range at the All-Star Game. The area around the players is blocked off since there are so many VIPs and such a large media presence, to say nothing of security. You generally can't go to the lower concourse without the right ticket, either. So leave your balls at home, just make sure to bring them to Fan Fest!

There have been many great moments over the years at the All-Star games, and we hope to attend more of them for a chance at glimpsing history. For example, on the fiftieth anniversary of the first All-Star game, Fred Lynn hit the first grand slam in All-Star history! And no one would be surprised that, in that first All-Star game in Chicago, Babe Ruth was the first to hit a home run. Putting the best of the best into one game, for the joy of baseball itself, creates great moments. We look forward to the next one after we publish this book...the All-Star game in our own ballpark home, Petco Park in San Diego.

There are season ticket holder perks if the All-Star Game is being held at your stadium. There are volunteer opportunities as well, where season ticket holders can work a shift manning a booth or handing out schedules, and then get free or discounted access to all the exhibits, and also get a collectible jersey, hat, backpack, and so on. This is something for you diehard fans to keep in mind! We'll certainly be checking into it—what a great opportunity to be able to help your favorite players!

The Midsummer Classic has a great atmosphere. The crowd is just so happy for the game. There are no team loyalties, no bad will; it is baseball in its purist form. The players are smiling, the crowd is roaring, and all that matters is hearing the crack of a hit ball and seeing the dirt coating a player's jersey after a diving catch. When we asked Grant about a special moment from our entire trip that stood out to him, he said it was when the crowd started chanting for Derek Jeter at the All-Star game. We all agree this is a great choice for a favorite moment. It gave us all chills! A memory we will never forget!

During the game, as an additional farewell to Jeter, a very moving ad was played on the big screen. It was a Nike commercial, and in it, Jeter steps up to the plate. He tips the lid of his batting helmet in a signature gesture, and raises the bat to his shoulder. He is given a respectful tip back from the pitcher. From there, we see important figures like Michael Jordan and Rudy Giuliani tipping their hats to Jeter, all over the country. It was very moving, and at times a bit funny, like when the Mets' players (rivals of Jeter's Yankee team) tip their hats, their faces blurred out for anonymity's sake. At that moment, Mr. Met, the Mets' mascot for over forty years, leans into the scene and tips his, his face uselessly blurred. It was a very nice thing to see, and there weren't that many dry eyes in the house afterwards. Jeter was such an iconic gentleman and respected player throughout his career, and we feel very lucky that we've been able to see him play. When Jeter was relieved in the fourth inning and left to that third standing ovation, it was an awe-inspiring moment, and it will always stand out as one of the highlights of our journey.

Despite the preponderance of goodwill at the All-Star Game, there is still something at stake that is very important later on: home field advantage in the World Series. One thing we learned over our journey is that while the home team doesn't always win, the home crowd is always a factor. In recent World Series, the home team has a very good record, and over the past thirty years there have been only a handful of series victories for the visiting team.

Minneapolis is definitely a city we would love to revisit. The stadium was great, and we didn't get to do too much out and about in the area, as this was one of those weekends dominated by baseball. Saturday and Sunday were spent enjoying Fan Fest before the big crowds,

Monday was the Home Run Derby, and Tuesday was the All-Star Game. We headed home tired, proud, and fulfilled—we had completed the journey, just like we had promised ourselves!

We hope this will become something that stays with our family, and that the boys and their families will continue to enjoy our great national pastime. This has certainly become an official Haferkamp tradition. Steve and Dayna even talk about working at spring training after retirement!

You can even start out small! We went to some minor league games in Jupiter that were a ton of fun. Minor league games are a great option for families just getting into baseball for a number of reasons. You generally get a lot of the perks of spring training games: tickets are cheaper, games tend to be very exciting, and the crowds are smaller, and so on. Many games also feature a fun activity between each inning where they need people from the crowd...spinning around with your head on the bat, kids rolling five big dice to win a prize, stuff like that. Minor league games are appealing to kids. College games are another great way to enjoy a game of baseball, and can offer up unique opportunities. For example, Grant wouldn't have the connection he does with Kris Bryant if it weren't for the fact that we went to college games. Grant has enjoyed playing for the North County Mavericks developmental team for many years, one of the founders of which, Coach Brad Marcelino, is batting coach for USD. It was because of this connection that we ended up going to several USD games. Ultimately this led to Grant being bat boy there, where he met Bryant well before his professional career had started. So start off small, and soon you might find yourselves on a quest to hit 'em all!

Over the course of our trip, we've learned many things. We've learned not to be disappointed if a game gets rained out, because you never know what the next game might bring. We've realized how important it is to get to games early, stay late, and make the most of our time. We've learned an incredible amount of baseball history, as so many of these wonderful stadiums have extensive museums, halls of fame, and memorial statues. Baseball can be a slow game, but it is an incredibly rich one, and can offer sudden spectacles out of the most normal of events.

You never know when you are going to see a record-breaking home run, a fantastic diving catch, or a no-hitter.

We've become pros at navigating crowds, meeting players, getting autographs, and making connections both on and off the field. We have been guided by our own "Angels in the Outfield" and our "Clubhouse Heroes," those exceptional folks who make going to games such a wonderful experience. We've watched our ball, card, bat, and bobblehead collections grow, despite the occasional toddler-related disaster. In fact, our baseball skills may have even gotten a little better too!

We've learned that good things come to those who wait, and that being generous, patient, and polite pays off. We've learned that sometimes, you just need to be in the right place at the right time, whether it's for snagging a home run ball or meeting one of the baseball greats. We've seen thrilling victories and heartbreaking defeats, and moments where competition is transcended by brotherly love and the bonds of a shared passion. We've seen players and teams rise and fall, and realize that no victory is perfect and no loss is permanent.

It was a great family adventure, and something we will never forget. Baseball brought us closer together, and will be a part of a family forever. Nothing compares to the thrill of a ballgame. You get to see a very important cultural slice of each city; you smell and taste the food, hear the sounds, and breathe the air of a city with its own history, stories, and love for the game. It was fun, most definitely, but it was also a learning experience. We learned more than we expected to, and look forward to experiencing the little things, and meeting the players, that we missed the first time around.

We really hope that this book will inspire you to take a journey of your own to see what the stadiums and cities of MLB have to offer, and that we have offered a few useful tips that will come in handy. It was truly a life-changing experience, and we have come out of it with a wealth of memories. From that first moment when we would all step off an airplane in a new place everything was always so exciting! Checking into a hotel, seeing new cities, people and views, waking up the day of the game...we loved every minute of it! These baseball stadiums have become our home away from home.

We love the game of baseball, and can't think of a better way to spend time with family than by settling into our seats, with the smell of popcorn and hotdogs wafting in the air, while listening to vendors yell, "Get your peanuts and Cracker Jacks!" as the announcer proudly gives the names of the stars that will wow thousands of fans over the course of an afternoon. There is truly nothing quite like the anticipation of hearing those two words everyone is waiting to hear, and every baseball fan would love to say..."Play ball!"

It's supposed to be fun, the man says "Play Ball," not "Work Ball," you know.

-Willie Stargell

Bibliography

Over the course of our journey, we learned quite a bit about baseball history. The museums that can be found scattered across North American ballparks are an incredible resource. While writing this book, we found the following books to be a fantastic supplement to the educational portions of the trip. If you would like to find out more about the American Association, defunct parks, or how spring training came to be, we highly recommend them!

Appel, Marty. *Pinstripe Empire: The New York Yankees from Before the Babe to After the Boss.* New York: Bloomsbury USA, 2012.

Armour, Mark. *Rain Check: Baseball in the Pacific Northwest.* Phoenix, Arizona: Society for American Baseball Research, 2006.

Buckley, James. *America's Classic Ballparks.* San Diego: Thunder Bay Press, 2013.

Fountain, Charles. *The Betrayal: The 1919 World Series and the Birth of Modern Baseball.* Oxford: Oxford University Press, 2015.

Fountain, Charles. *Under the March Sun: The Story of Spring Training.* Oxford: Oxford University Press, 2009.

Magee, David, and Shirley, Philip. *Sweet Spot: 125 Years of Baseball and the Louisville Slugger*. Chicago: Triumph Books, 2009.

Maraniss, David. *Clemente: The Passion and Grace of Baseball's Last Hero* by David Maraniss. New York: Simon and Schuster, 2007.

McCollister, John, and Tekulve, Kent. *The Bucs!: The Story of the Pittsburgh Pirates*. Lanham, Maryland: Taylor Trade Publishing, 1998.

National Baseball Hall of Fame. *Baseball as America: Seeing Ourselves through Our National Game*. Washington, D.C.: National Geographic, 2002.

Nemec, David. *The Beer and Whisky League: The Illustrated History of the American Association-Baseball's Renegade Major League*. Guilford, Connecticut: Lyons Press, 2004.

Pahigian, Josh, and O'Connell, Kevin. *The Ultimate Baseball Road Trip: A Fan's Guide to Major League Stadiums*. Guilford, Connecticut: Lyons Press, 2004.

Schwarz, Alan, and Gammons, Peter. *The Numbers Game: Baseball's Lifelong Fascination with Statistics*. New York: St. Martin's Griffin, 2005.

Smith, Ron. *The Ballpark Book: A Journey through the Fields of Baseball Magic*. New York: McGraw Hill, 2000.

Swank, Bill. *Baseball in San Diego: From the Plaza to the Padres*. Mount Pleasant, South Carolina: Arcadia Publishing, 2004.

Zachofsky, Dan. *Collecting Baseball Memorabilia: A Handbook*. Jefferson, North Carolina: McFarland, 2009.

Our All-Star Roster

As they say, there is no "I" in "team!"

To our sons, Grant and Jack, who lived and breathed this incredible journey: we are so very proud of you! We appreciate all your hard work and contributions to the book. We love your passion for the game, watching you play baseball & most importantly being good teammates.

To our parents, Don and Della and Clay and Carmen, we feel blessed for your unwavering love and support. To our entire family; Dean, Deanna and Joel, Donell, Robbie, Rikki and Stuart, Dixie and Frank, Lauren, Danny & Georgia, Erin and Brian, Cristen and Josh, Donnie and Kathy, Molly, Clay, the Vaccaro and Schaffnit families. You've been an outstanding clubhouse, and as we say in the Burgh, "We are Family!" ...and proud of it.

Many thanks also to Bud Black, our inspiration and skipper along this journey! You made such a difference in our life from the very first day we met you. We will be forever grateful. It was your incredible impression that forged our love of the game, and it will be passed on to others.

To our dear circle of friends, you know who you are! We consider you our West Coast family. Our baseball community, the LCYO Rebel Families, the North County Mavericks, Encinitas National Little League, and all the great baseball coaches who have taught our boys to respect the game and play it the right way.

We would also like to thank Clint Hurdle. You are truly an inspiration to our family and others. We feel honored to receive your daily "Make a difference today, love, Clint" messages...it brings us such joy. "Raise the Jolly Roger!"

Mark "Mud" Grant, you are an amazing commentator, who relates so well with the fans of the game. "Win or lose," you always put a smile on our faces.

Coach Robinson, you and Beverly are both "Hall of Famers" in our book. You have touched the lives of many and we are so proud to call you our friends!

Matt Vasgersian, "The Voice of Baseball," heard by millions, thank you for embracing our journey and sharing your insight. You are the first voice we hear every morning as the kids are playing *MLB the Show* or watching *MLB Network*.

Coach Kevin O'Sullivan, we are thankful and amazed that the great game of baseball can reconnect two people after twenty-five years. Go Gators!

Our profound gratitude also goes out to Coach Brad, Ray Fosse, Coach Machado, Coach Possemato, Coach Lavoie, Chad Moeller, Coach Dale, Coach Gene, Bob Bray, Donna Mangold, Coach Hargrave, Kono Blackburn, Jerry Hairston Jr., Steve Carter, Coach Erik, Mark Sweeney, Coach Hayes, Kyle Phillips, Debbie Cunningham, Melanie Lenz, Coach Kirk, David Rinetti, Pete Leddy, Alan Andrew, Bret Alexander, Coach Jay, Rick Redman, and Mrs. Bob Shaw.

Our MLB baseball friends who taught us so much, and welcomed us into the "Big Leagues,"... Linda and Don, Terri, Austin, Brandon, and Tim.

MLB Commissioner, Robert D. Manfred Jr., your kind letter and encouragement to share our journey with others is a keepsake we will always treasure!

Our publisher, Mascot Books and the awesome team of Naren, Josh, Kristin, Ricky, and Chris.

To friends who supported and challenged Dayna to "put the ball in play" by writing this book: Jack, Kris, and Lea. Thank you for your encouragement!

To all of Dayna's wonderful colleagues, clients, and friends at Federated Investors. She is so proud to represent such a fine and reputable institution.

To friends in our home towns of Pittsburgh, Jupiter, and Denver. "This one's for the Home team!"

And to all those not mentioned who made our trip that much more magical for having been a part of it, thank you, and see you at the ball park!